Phonics
Consonants

Consonant Sounds
you need to know
to be a successful reader

Written by Shannon Keeley • Illustrated by Remy Simard

Flash Kids
A Division of Barnes & Noble
122 Fifth Avenue
New York, NY 10011

ISBN: 978-1-4114-9876-1

17 19 21 22 20 18 16

07/15

Please submit all inquiries to FlashKids@bn.com

Manufactured in Canada

Dear Parent,

Consonant letters are the building blocks of words. Knowing these letters and their sounds is an important step in learning to read. This book provides fun activities that introduce consonant letters and their sounds. The activities will help your child identify sounds that fall at the beginning and the end of words. Through tracing and writing, matching, games, mazes, and stories, your child will receive lots of practice distinguishing between the different consonant sounds. These activities build reading skills and give your child opportunities to decode words, phrases, and sentences. To get the most from the activities, follow these simple steps:

- Find a comfortable place where you and your child can work quietly together.

- Encourage your child to go at his or her own pace.

- Help your child if he or she gets stuck.

- Offer lots of praise and support.

- Most of all, remember that learning should be fun! Take time to enjoy this special time spent together.

Visit us at *www.flashkidsbooks.com* for free downloads, informative articles, and valuable parent resources!

Alphabugs

Write the missing letters as you say the alphabet.

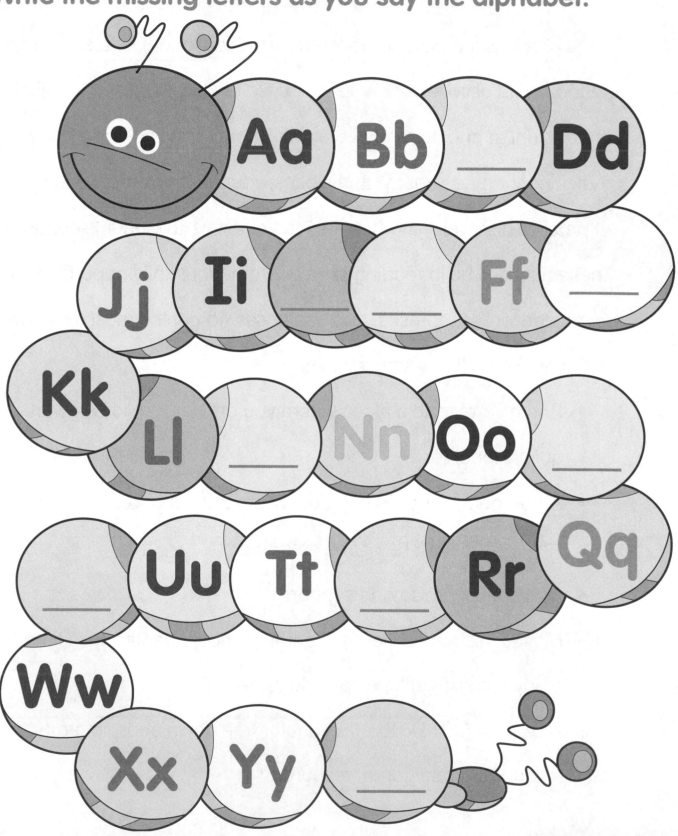

Aa Bb ___ Dd

Jj Ii ___ ___ Ff ___

Kk Ll ___ Nn Oo ___

___ Uu Tt ___ Rr Qq

Ww Xx Yy ___

Dot-to-Dot

Connect the dots from A to Z.

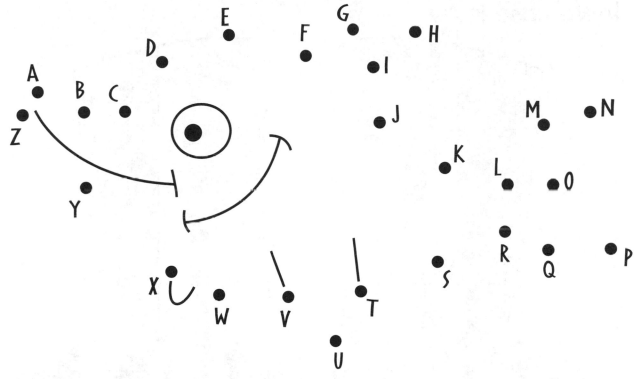

Connect the dots from a to z.

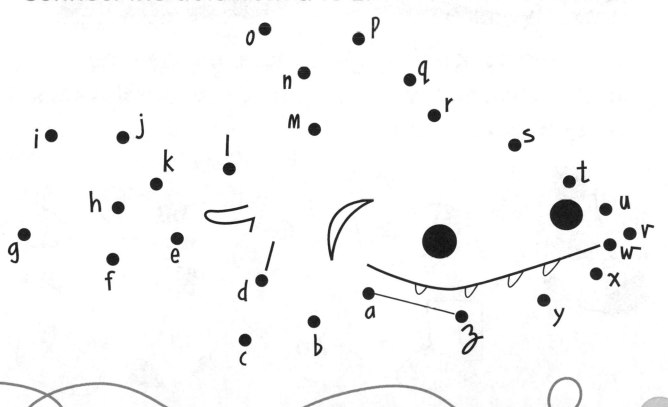

A Matching Pair

Connect each uppercase letter with its matching lowercase letter.

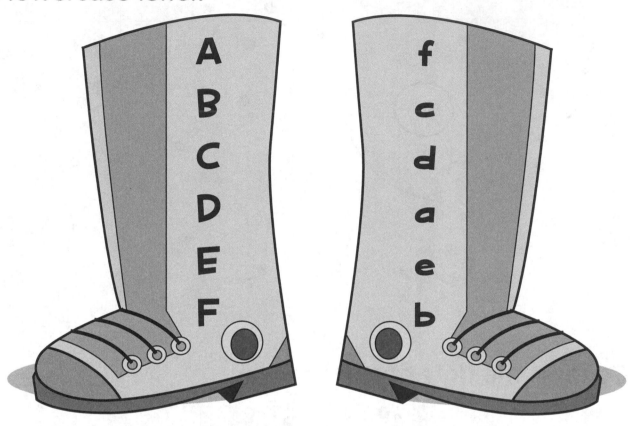

A B C D E F

f c d a e b

Circle the sock if the letters make a matching uppercase and lowercase pair. Cross out the sock if the letters don't match.

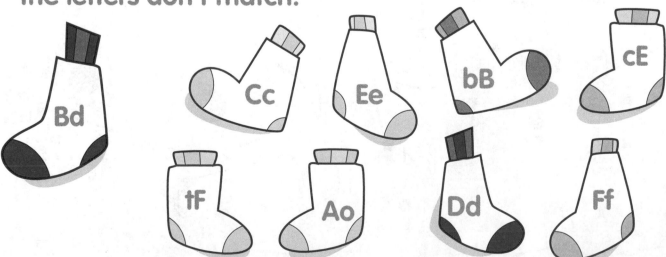

Bd   Cc   Ee   bB   cE

tF   Ao   Dd   Ff

Connect each uppercase letter with its matching lowercase letter.

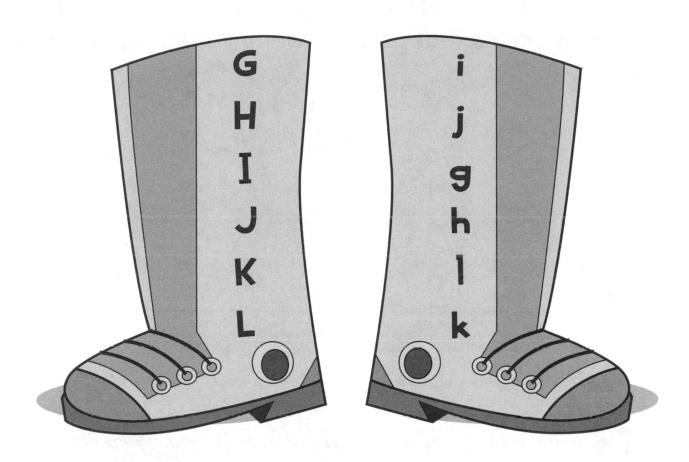

G H I J K L

i j g h l k

Circle the sock if the letters make a matching uppercase and lowercase pair. Cross out the sock if the letters don't match.

Li   hH   Kk   Ij   Gg

iI   jJ   Kx   lL

Letter Pair Popcorn

Which popcorn pieces belong in the box? Circle the popcorn pieces that go with the first letter in the row.

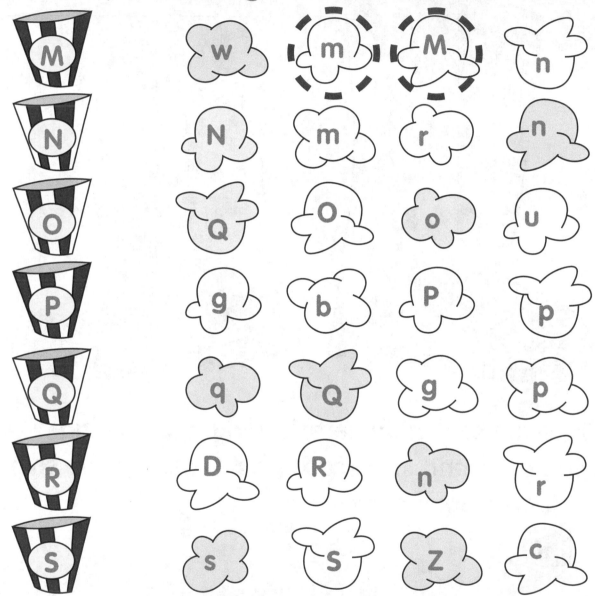

Now write the matching uppercase or lowercase letter.

M_____, _____ n, _____ o, P_____,

Q_____, _____ r, S_____

Which popcorn pieces belong in the box? Circle the popcorn pieces that go with the first letter in the row.

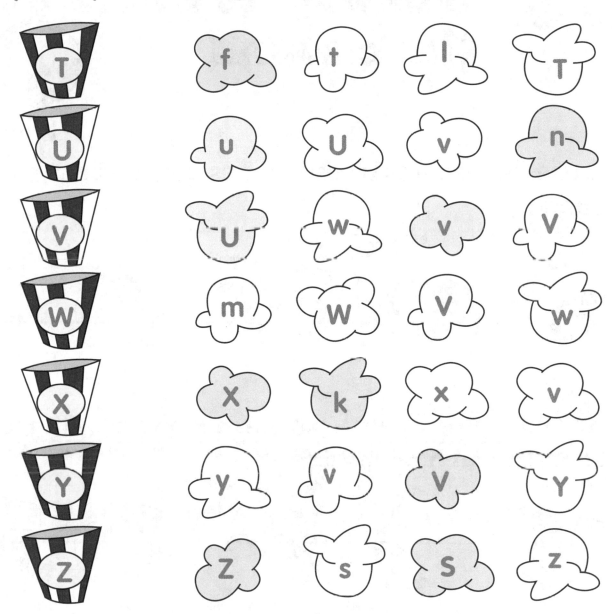

Now write the matching uppercase or lowercase letter.

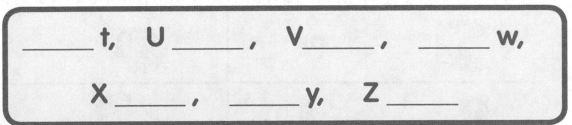

_____ t, U _____ , V _____ , _____ w,

X _____ , _____ y, Z _____

 **Ball begins with the b sound.**

ball

Circle the pictures whose names begin with the **b** sound.

Say the name of each picture. If it begins with the **b** sound, write **b** on the line.

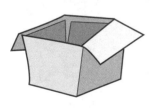    

_____   _____   _____   _____   _____

Write the beginning letter to complete each word.

 ____ox   ____un

 ____ell   ____ib

Tic-Tac-Toe

Circle the row whose pictures all begin with the **b** sound.

Circle the words that name the three pictures in the winning row.

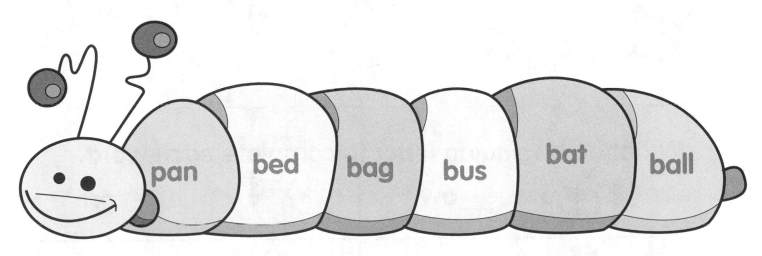

pan   bed   bag   bus   bat   ball

 # Cc Cat begins with the c sound.

cat

Circle the pictures whose names begin with the c sound.

Say the name of each picture. If it begins with the c sound, write c on the line.

  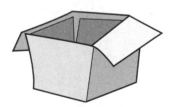  

_____   _____   _____   _____   _____

Write the beginning letter to complete each word.

 ___ow

 ___orn

 ___op

 ___oat

Maze Magic

Find your way through the maze! Connect the pictures whose names begin with c.

Which pictures did you connect in the maze? Circle the words that name those pictures.

cow　　cup　　car　　corn　　cat

Dog begins with the d sound.

dog

Circle the pictures whose names begin with the d sound.

  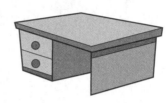 

Say the name of each picture. If it begins with the d sound, write d on the line.

_____ _____ _____ _____ _____

Write the beginning letter to complete each word.

 _____inner

 _____ish

 _____own

 _____ig

Hidden Picture

Say the name of each picture. If it begins with the d sound, color the space.

Look at the pictures in the spaces you colored. Circle the words that name those pictures.

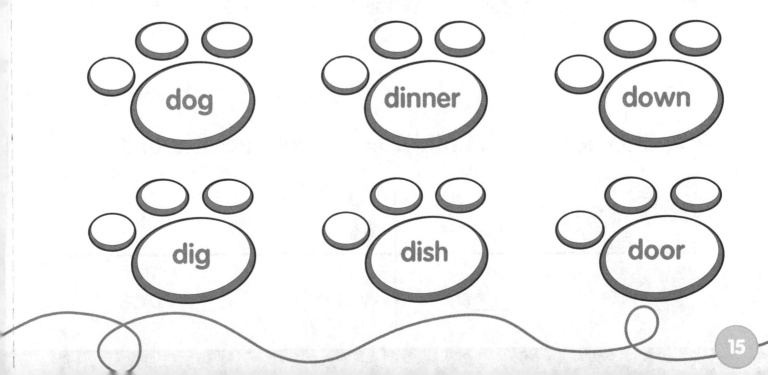

dog   dinner   down

dig   dish   door

 # Ff

Fish begins with the f sound.

fish

Circle the pictures whose names begin with the **f** sound.

Say the name of each picture. If it begins with the **f** sound, write **f** on the line.

_____   _____   _____   _____   _____

Write the beginning letter to complete each word.

 _____og

 _____all

 _____at

 _____ace

Teamwork

Circle the pictures whose names begin with the **f** sound. Count the number and write it below the team. The team with the highest number wins!

Team A:

Team B:

Let's Review

Say the name of the first picture in each row. Circle the pictures in the row that have the same beginning sound.

1.

2.

3.

4.

Write the letter for the beginning sound of each word.

1. _____

2. _____

3. _____

4. _____

Word Wagons

Circle the correct word for each picture.

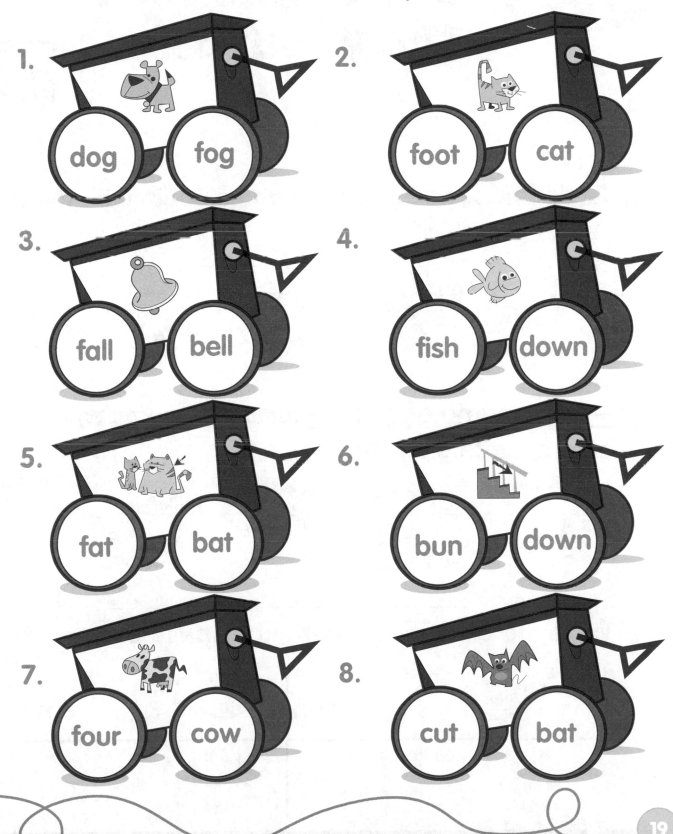

1. dog | fog

2. foot | cat

3. fall | bell

4. fish | down

5. fat | bat

6. bun | down

7. four | cow

8. cut | bat

Gg

Gas begins with the g sound.

gas

Circle the pictures whose names begin with the **g** sound.

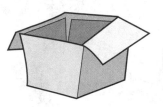    

Say the name of each picture. If it begins with the **g** sound, write **g** on the line.

_____   _____   _____   _____   _____

Write the beginning letter to complete each word.

 _____arden

 _____ame

 _____irl

 _____o

Tic-Tac-Toe

Circle the row whose pictures all begin with the **g** sound.

Circle the words that name the three pictures in the winning row.

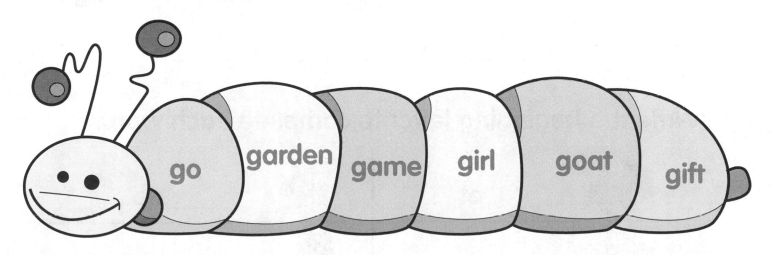

go garden game girl goat gift

Hh Hat begins with the h sound.

hat

Circle the pictures whose names begin with the h sound.

Say the name of each picture. If it begins with the h sound, write **h** on the line.

_____ _____ _____ _____ _____

Write the beginning letter to complete each word.

 _____ot

 _____op

 _____ug

 _____ole

Maze Magic

Find your way through the maze! Connect the pictures whose names begin with **h**.

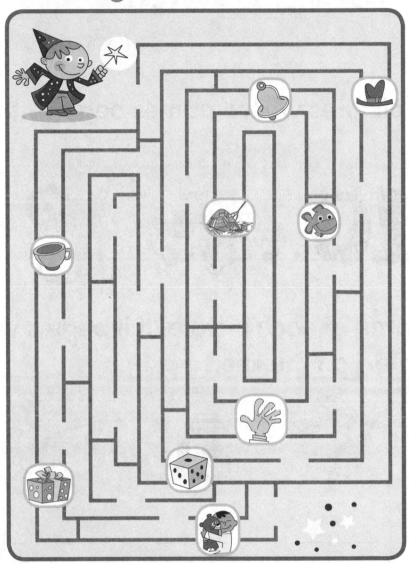

Which pictures did you connect in the maze? Circle the words that name those pictures.

hand   hay   hill   hat   hug

Jj

Jug begins with the j sound.

jug

Circle the pictures whose names begin with the **j** sound.

Say the name of each picture. If it begins with the **j** sound, write **j** on the line.

_____   _____   _____

Write the beginning letter to complete each word.

 _____acket

 _____ump

 _____ungle

 _____ail

Hidden Picture

Say the name of each picture. If it begins with the **j** sound, color the space.

Look at the pictures in the spaces you colored. Circle the words that name those pictures.

jacket juggle jump

jet jeans jam

Kk

Key begins with the k sound.

key

Circle the pictures whose names begin with the k sound.

Say the name of each picture. If it begins with the k sound, write k on the line.

_____ _____ _____ _____ _____

Write the beginning letter to complete each word.

 ___id

 ___ick

 ___itten

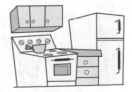 ___itchen

Teamwork

Circle the pictures whose names begin with the k sound. Count the number and write it below the team. The team with the highest number wins!

Team A:

Team B:

Let's Review

Say the name of the first picture in each row. Circle the pictures in the row that have the same beginning sound.

Write the letter for the beginning sound of each word.

1. _____ 2. _____ 3. _____ 4. _____

Word Wagons

Circle the correct word for each picture.

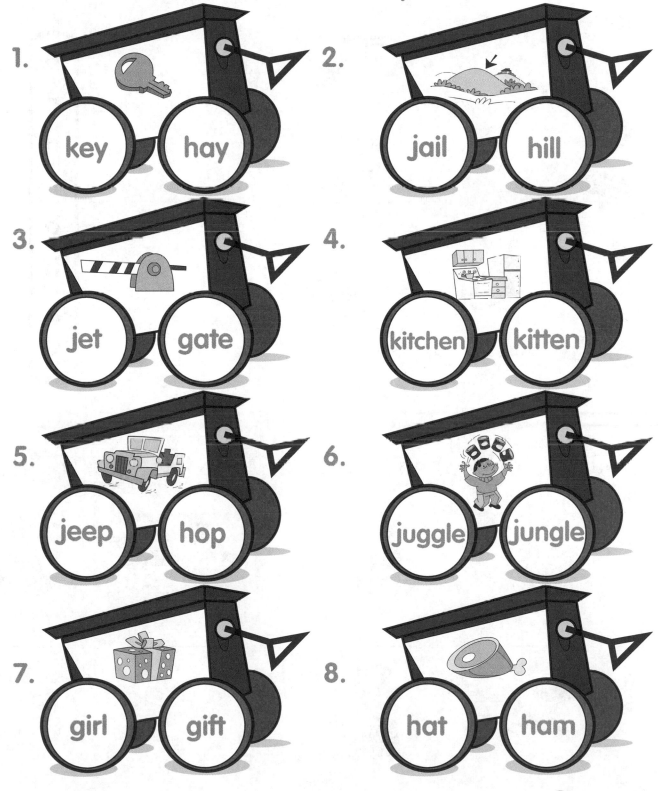

1. key   hay

2. jail   hill

3. jet   gate

4. kitchen   kitten

5. jeep   hop

6. juggle   jungle

7. girl   gift

8. hat   ham

Let's Review

Connect each picture with the letter for the beginning sound.

b
c
d
f
g
h
j
k

Say the name of each picture. Write the letter for the beginning sound.

1.
_____

2. 4
_____

3.
_____

4.
_____

5.
_____

6.
_____

7.
_____

8.
_____

Bows and Hats

Draw a line from each word to the picture it names.

cat
kite

dog
fog

corn
horse

bus
gas

Circle the name of each picture.

1.

fall   jail

2.

bag   dig

3.

desk   kiss

4.

goat   coat

5.

car   jar

6.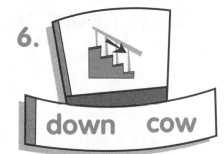

down   cow

31

Picture This

Read each phrase and draw a line to the matching picture.

1. a bag of corn

2. a jar of dice

3. a big gift

4. a hot dinner

5. five keys

6. a cup of juice

a)

b)

c)

d)

e)

f)

Now read the phrase and draw your own picture.

a cow on a hill

Read and Number

Read each sentence and find the matching picture.
Write the number by the sentence.

The kangaroo can hop. _____
I put gas in the bus. _____
I juggle four cans. _____
The fish is on the dish. _____

1.

2.

3.

4.

Lunch begins with the *l* sound.

lunch

Circle the pictures whose names begin with the l sound.

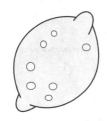    

Say the name of each picture. If it begins with the l sound, write l on the line.

 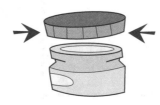  

_____   _____   _____   _____   _____

Write the beginning letter to complete each word.

 ____ap   ____ick

 ____ist    ____ine

Tic-Tac-Toe

Circle the row whose pictures all begin with the l sound.

Circle the words that name the three pictures in the winning row.

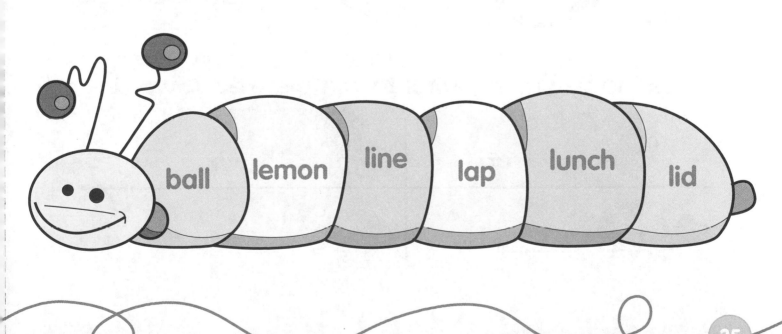

ball lemon line lap lunch lid

Mm

Milk begins with the m sound.

milk

Circle the pictures whose names begin with the m sound.

Say the name of each picture. If it begins with the m sound, write m on the line.

_____   _____   _____   _____   _____

Write the beginning letter to complete each word.

 ____ad

 ____ix

 ____ud

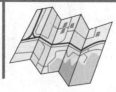 ____ap

Maze Magic

Find your way through the maze! Connect the pictures whose names begin with **m**.

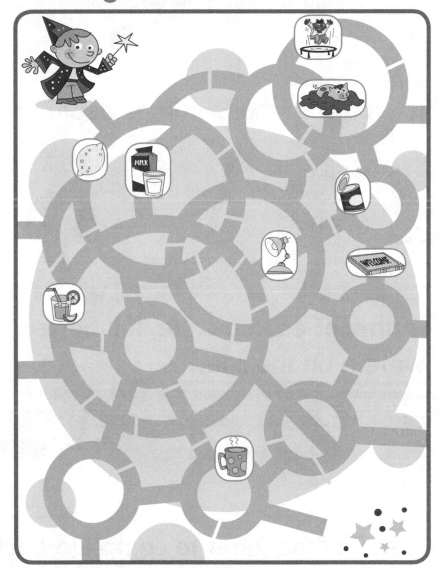

Which pictures did you connect in the maze? Circle the words that name those pictures.

mud   milk   mad   mug   mat

 **Net begins with the n sound.**

net

Circle the pictures whose names begin with the n sound.

    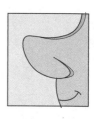

Say the name of each picture. If it begins with the n sound, write n on the line.

_____   _____   _____   _____

Write the beginning letter to complete each word.

 _____ap

 _____oon

 _____urse

 _____ut

Hidden Picture

Say the name of each picture. If it begins with the **n** sound, color the space.

Look at the pictures in the spaces you colored. Circle the words that name those pictures.

nose   nine   nurse   nap   noon   nail

Pan begins with the p sound.

pan

Circle the pictures whose names begin with the p sound.

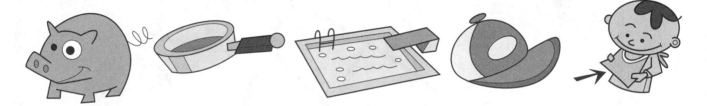

Say the name of each picture. If it begins with the p sound, write p on the line.

  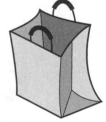

_____   _____   _____   _____   _____

Write the beginning letter to complete each word.

____in   ____ants

____aw   ____ull

Teamwork

Circle the pictures whose names begin with the p sound. Count the number and write it below the team. The team with the highest number wins!

Team A:

Team B:

Let's Review

Say the name of the first picture in each row. Circle the pictures in the row that have the same beginning sound.

Write the letter for the beginning sound of each word.

1. _____ 2. _____ 3. _____ 4. _____

Word Wagons

Circle the correct word for each picture.

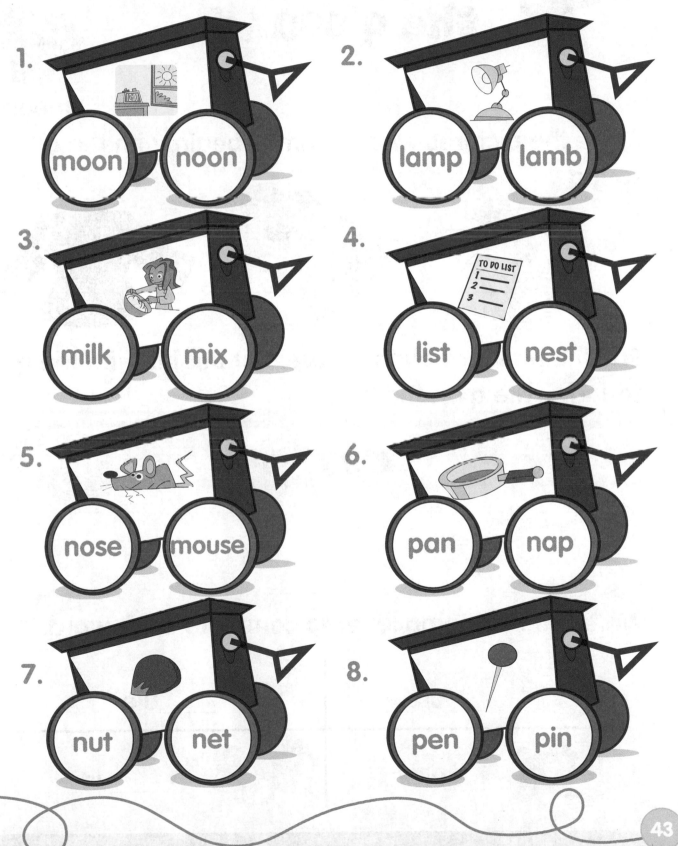

1. moon / noon

2. lamp / lamb

3. milk / mix

4. list / nest

5. nose / mouse

6. pan / nap

7. nut / net

8. pen / pin

 **Queen begins with the q sound.**

queen

Circle the pictures whose names begin with the **q** sound.

Say the name of each picture. If it begins with the **q** sound, write **q** on the line.

_____   _____   _____

Write the beginning letter to complete each word.

 ____uiz

 ____uiet

 ____uick

 ____uit

Tic-Tac-Toe

Circle the row whose pictures all begin with the **q** sound.

Circle the words that name the three pictures in the winning row.

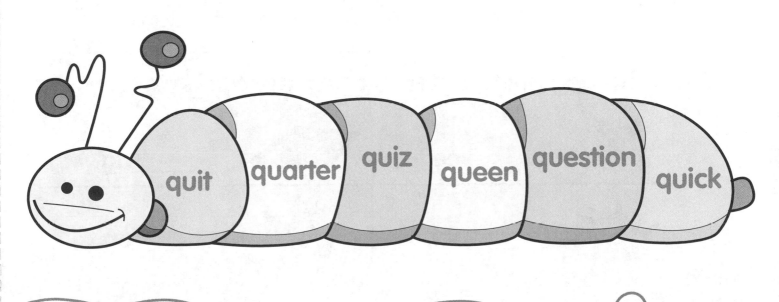

quit   quarter   quiz   queen   question   quick

 **Rr**

Rat begins with the r sound.

rat

Circle the pictures whose names begin with the r sound.

Say the name of each picture. If it begins with the r sound, write r on the line.

_____   _____   _____   _____   _____

Write the beginning letter to complete each word.

 _____ice

 _____ug

 _____ock

 _____un

Maze Magic

Find your way through the maze! Connect the pictures whose names begin with r.

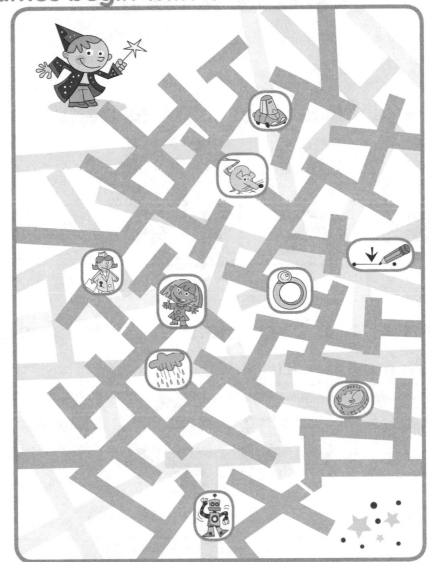

Which pictures did you connect in the maze? Circle the words that name those pictures.

rain · robot · rat · ring · rock

Ss

sock begins with the s sound.

sock

Circle the pictures whose names begin with the **s** sound.

Say the name of each picture. If it begins with the **s** sound, write **s** on the line.

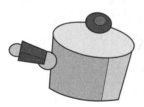    

_____   _____   _____   _____   _____

Write the beginning letter to complete each word.

 _____ad

 _____alt

 _____and

 _____ing

48

Hidden Picture

Say the name of each picture. If it begins with the **s** sound, color the space.

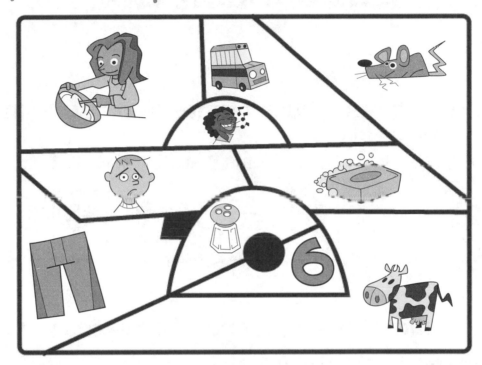

Look at the pictures in the spaces you colored. Circle the words that name those pictures.

six   sing   soap

salt   sand   sad

Tt

Tub begins with the t sound.

tub

Circle the pictures whose names begin with the t sound.

Say the name of each picture. If it begins with the t sound, write t on the line.

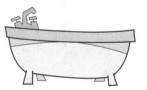

_____   _____   _____   _____   _____

Write the beginning letter to complete each word.

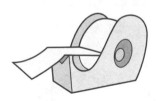 _____ag

 _____oys

 _____ooth

 _____op

Teamwork

Circle the pictures whose names begin with the t sound. Count the number and write it below the team. The team with the highest number wins!

Team A:

Team B:

Let's Review

Say the name of the first picture in each row. Circle the pictures in the row that have the same beginning sound.

Write the letter for the beginning sound of each word.

1. _____ 2. _____ 3. _____ 4. _____

Word Wagons

Circle the correct word for each picture.

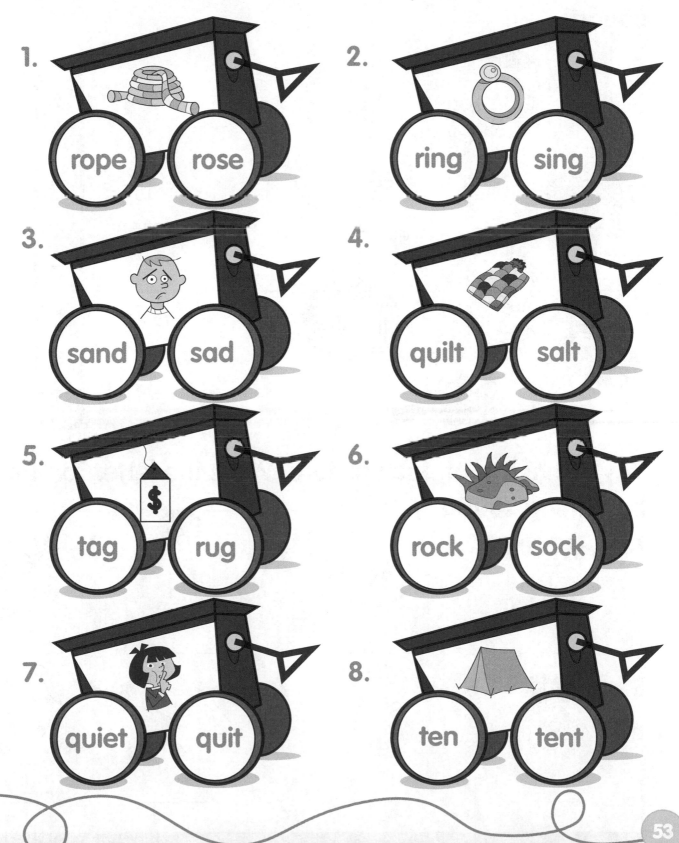

1. rope   rose

2. ring   sing

3. sand   sad

4. quilt   salt

5. tag   rug

6. rock   sock

7. quiet   quit

8. ten   tent

Let's Review

Connect each picture with the letter for the beginning sound.

Say the name of each picture. Write the letter for the beginning sound.

1.  2. 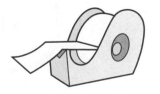 3.   4.

_____   _____   _____   _____

5.  6.  7.  8.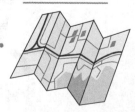

_____   _____   _____   _____

Bows and Hats

Draw a line from each word to the picture it names.

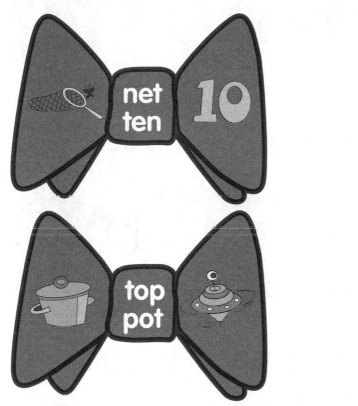

net
ten

10

nine
rain

9

top
pot

lake
quilt

Circle the name of each picture.

1.

mix   six

2.

top   mop

3.

nose rose

4.

queen   pen

5.

saw   paw

6.

mug   rug

55

 **van begins with the v sound.**

van

Circle the pictures whose names begin with the v sound.

Say the name of each picture. If it begins with the v sound, write v on the line.

_____   _____   _____

Write the beginning letter to complete each word.

 ____egetables   ____ine

 ____est    ____olleyball

Tic-Tac-Toe

Circle the row whose pictures all begin with the v sound.

Circle the words that name the three pictures in the winning row.

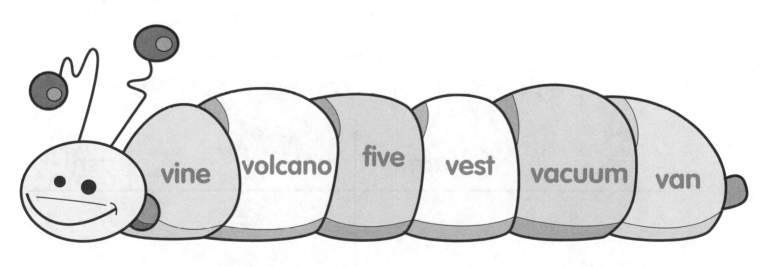

vine   volcano   five   vest   vacuum   van

 **Wet begins with the w sound.**

wet

Circle the pictures whose names begin with the **w** sound.

 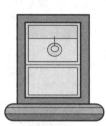  

Say the name of each picture. If it begins with the **w** sound, write **w** on the line.

_____ _____ _____ _____ _____

Write the beginning letter to complete each word.

 _____arm

 _____ash

 _____ave

 _____ind

Maze Magic

Find your way through the maze! Connect the pictures whose names begin with **w**.

Which pictures did you connect in the maze? Circle the words that name those pictures.

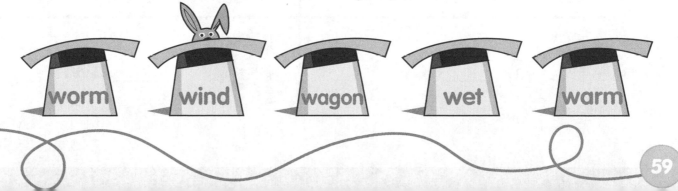

worm   wind   wagon   wet   warm

Yy

Yo-yo begins with the y sound.

yo-yo

Circle the pictures whose names begin with the y sound.

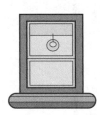    

Say the name of each picture. If it begins with the y sound, write y on the line.

_____   _____   _____   _____   _____

Write the beginning letter to complete each word.

 _____ellow

 _____ell

 _____ear

 _____awn

60

Hidden Picture

Say the name of each picture. If it begins with the y sound, color the space.

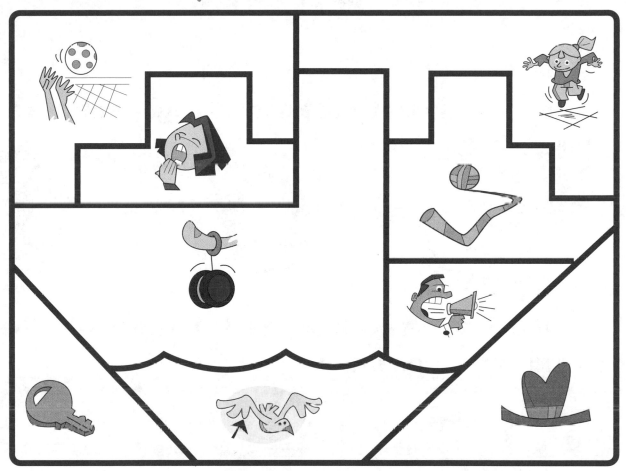

Look at the pictures in the spaces you colored. Circle the words that name those pictures.

van   year   yarn

yo-yo   yell   yawn

 **Zz** **zebra begins with the z sound.**

zebra

Circle the pictures whose names begin with the **z** sound.

Say the name of each picture. If it begins with the **z** sound, write **z** on the line.

_____ _____ _____

Write the beginning letter to complete each word.

 _____oo

 _____ero

 _____ipper

 _____ig zag

Teamwork

Circle the pictures whose names begin with the **z** sound. Count the number and write it below the team. The team with the highest number wins!

Team A:

Team B:

Let's Review

Say the name of the first picture in each row. Circle the pictures in the row that have the same beginning sound.

Write the letter for the beginning sound of each word.

1. _____ 2. _____ 3. _____ 4. _____

Word Wagons

Circle the correct word for each picture.

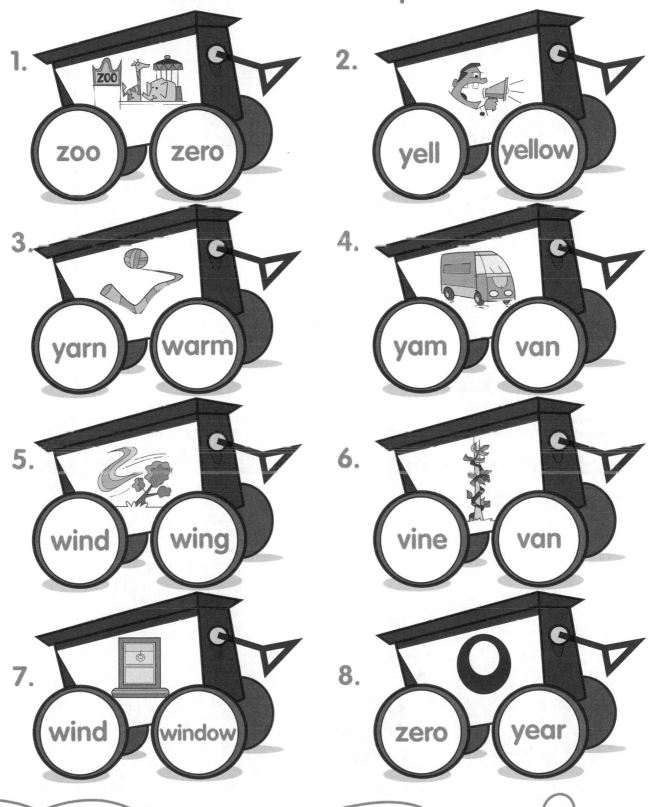

1. zoo   zero

2. yell   yellow

3. yarn   warm

4. yam   van

5. wind   wing

6. vine   van

7. wind   window

8. zero   year

Let's Review

Connect each picture with the letter for the beginning sound.

q
r
s
t
v
w
y
z

Say the name of each picture. Write the letter for the beginning sound.

1.

2.

3.

4.

5.

6.

7.

8.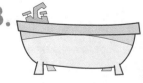

Bows and Hats

Draw a line from each word to the picture it names.

quit
wet

quiz
zero

year
rain

toys
yo-yo

Circle the name of each picture.

1.

toe   zoo

2.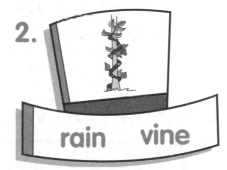

rain   vine

3.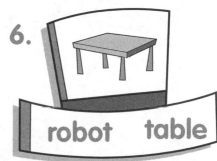

zipper   soap

4.

worm   year

5.

rat   vest

6.

robot   table

Picture This

Read each phrase and draw a line to the matching picture.

1. a sad queen

2. pens in a mug

3. ten nails

4. warm rice

5. six yellow lemons

6. zip the tent

a)

b)

c)

d)

e)

f)

Now read the phrase and draw your own picture.

a pail in the rain

Read and Number

Read each sentence and find the matching picture.
Write the number by the sentence.

I had vegetables and milk for lunch. _____
The zebra is quick. _____
A pool is in the yard. _____
We wash the van. _____

Picture Search

Read the words in the box. Find each word in the picture. Write each word on the correct line.

| ball | coat | duck | fish | girl |
| hat | jeep | lake | map | kite |

mug   net   pail   quilt   tent

van   wolf   yo-yo   sand   zip

Story Time

Read the story. Write the correct word from the box to complete each sentence.

king	milk
queen	bug
noon	

1. Lunch is at _____.

2. The _____ has vegetables.

3. The _____ has yams.

4. The cat has _____.

5. A _____ hops.

juice door
pool wet
table

6. It zig zags on the _____.

7. The _____ falls.

8. They are sad and _____.

9. They run out the _____.

10. They go in the _____.

Circle the Sentence

Circle the sentence that matches the picture.

1.

a) The dog licks my face.

b) The dog kicks my face

2.

a) I wash my ham in the sink.

b) I wash my hands in the sink.

3.

a) The kid has a quilt at his desk.

b) The kid has a quiz at his desk.

4.

a) I see a goat at the zoo.

b) I see a pot at the zoo.

Who's Who?

Read each sentence. Who does it describe? Write the name by the correct picture.

Rob the cop has a rose.
Mark has mud on his jeans.
Amy the nurse has yogurt.
Pete the pig is in the tub.
Jill vacuums under the bed.

1.

_____

2.

_____

3.

_____

4.

_____

5.

_____

Bb

Tub ends with the b sound.

web

Circle the pictures whose names end with the b sound.

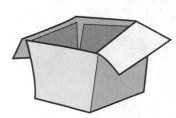 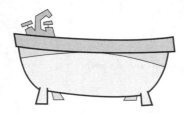  

Say the name of each picture. If it ends with the b sound, write b on the line.

_____   _____   _____   _____

Write the ending letter to complete each word.

  cra_____ | 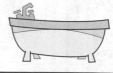 tu_____

 ru_____ |  bi_____

Tic-Tac-Toe

Circle the row whose pictures all end with the **b** sound.

Circle the words that name the three pictures in the winning row.

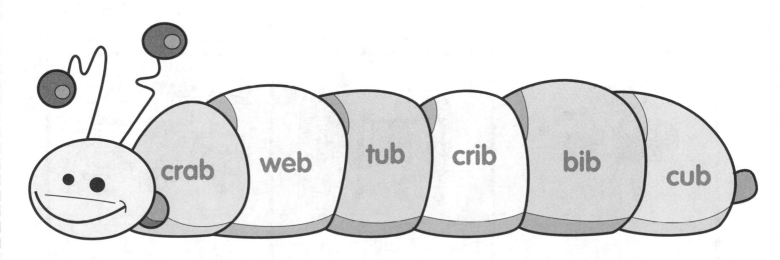

crab   web   tub   crib   bib   cub

Left or Right?

Say the name of each picture. If the word begins with the b sound, write b on the left line. If it ends with the b sound, write b on the right line.

Draw a Line

Say the name of each picture. Draw a line to match each picture with the correct sign.

Beginning
b sound

Ending
b sound

Dd

Hood ends with the d sound.

hood

Circle the pictures whose names end with the **d** sound.

 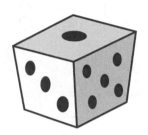  

Say the name of each picture. If it ends with the **d** sound, write **d** on the line.

_____   _____   _____   _____

Write the ending letter to complete each word.

 rea_____

 see_____

 woo_____

 foo_____

Maze Magic

Find your way through the maze! Connect the pictures whose names end with **d**.

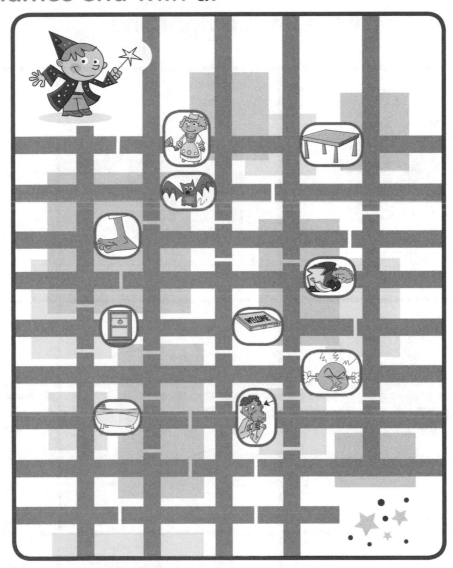

Which pictures did you connect in the maze? Circle the words that name those pictures.

food   wood   dad   maid   mad

Left or Right?

Say the name of each picture. If the word begins with the **d** sound, write **d** on the left line. If it ends with the **d** sound, write **d** on the right line.

Keep Track

Say the name of each picture in the race track. Count how many words begin with **d** and how many end with **d**. Write the numbers below. The higher number wins the race!

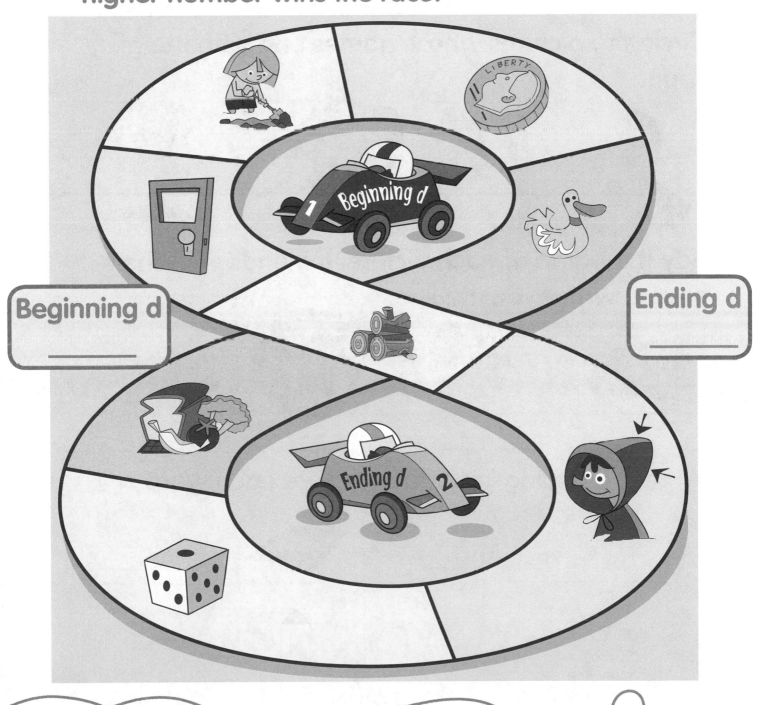

Beginning d
_____

Ending d
_____

Gg

Log ends with the g sound.

log

Circle the pictures whose names end with the g sound.

Say the name of each picture. If it ends with the g sound, write g on the line.

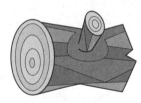   

_____ _____ _____ _____

Write the ending letter to complete each word.

 ju____

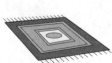 ru____

 jo____

 ta____

Hidden Picture

Say the name of each picture. If it ends with the **g** sound, color the space.

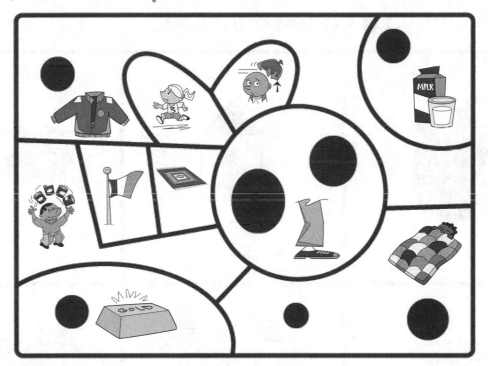

Look at the pictures in the spaces you colored. Circle the words that name those pictures.

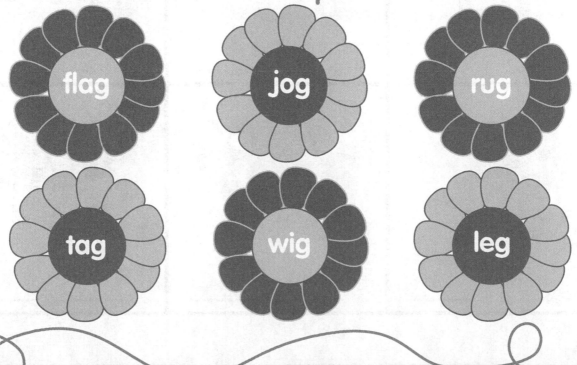

flag

jog

rug

tag

wig

leg

Left or Right?

Say the name of each picture. If the word begins with the **g** sound, write **g** on the left line. If it ends with the **g** sound, write **g** on the right line.

Connect Four

In each box, draw a line to connect the two pictures whose names begin with the **g** sound. Draw another line to connect those that end with the **g** sound.

 **Kk**

Book ends with the k sound.

book

Circle the pictures whose names end with the k sound.

Say the name of each picture. If it ends with the k sound, write k on the line.

_____ _____ _____ _____

Write the ending letter to complete each word.

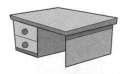 des_____

 loo_____

 pea_____

 wea_____

Teamwork

Circle the pictures whose names end with the k sound. Count the number and write it below the team. The team with the highest number wins!

Team A:

Team B:

Left or Right?

Say the name of each picture. If the word begins with the **k** sound, write **k** on the left line. If it ends with the **k** sound, write **k** on the right line.

Goal Time!

Say the name of each picture. Draw a line to connect each picture with the matching goal.

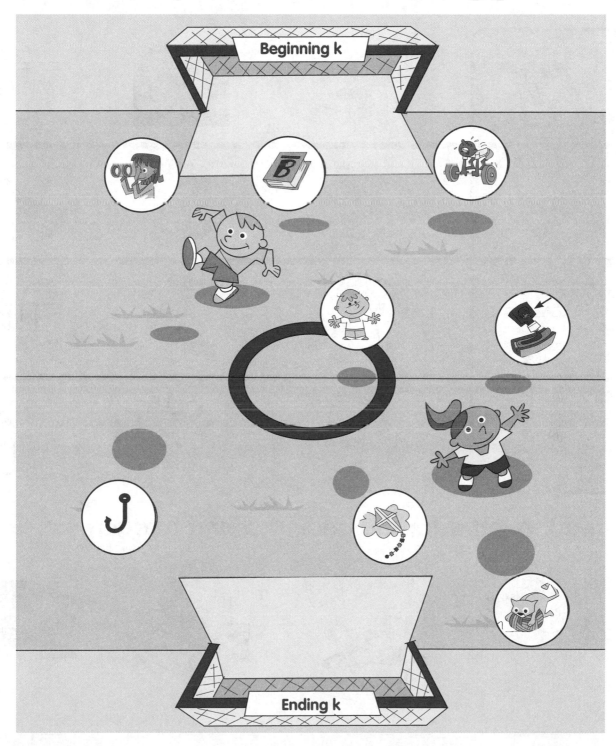

Let's Review

Say the name of the first picture in each row. Circle the pictures in the row that have the same ending sound.

Write the letter for the ending sound of each word.

1. _____ 2. _____ 3. _____ 4. _____

Word Wagons

Circle the correct word for each picture.

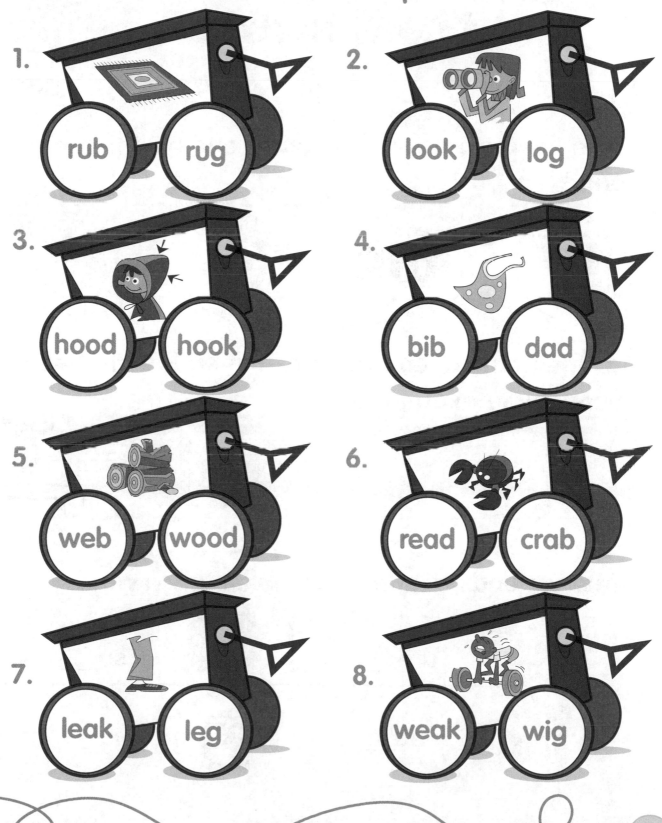

1. rub   rug

2. look   log

3. hood   hook

4. bib   dad

5. web   wood

6. read   crab

7. leak   leg

8. weak   wig

 **Mm**

Ham ends with the m sound.

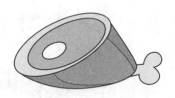

ham

Circle the pictures whose names end with the **m** sound.

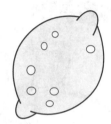   

Say the name of each picture. If it ends with the **m** sound, write **m** on the line.

  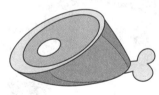 

_____   _____   _____   _____

Write the ending letter to complete each word.

   drea_____   su_____

   tea_____   ja_____

Tic-Tac-Toe

Circle the row whose pictures all end with the **m** sound.

Circle the words that name the three pictures in the winning row.

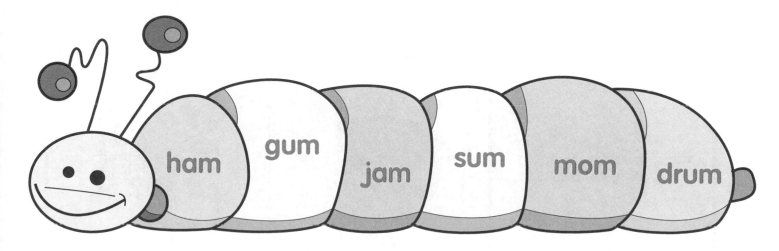

ham   gum   jam   sum   mom   drum

Left or Right?

Say the name of each picture. If the word begins with the **m** sound, write **m** on the left line. If it ends with the **m** sound, write **m** on the right line.

Draw a Line

Say the name of each picture. Draw a line to match each picture with the correct sign.

Beginning m sound

Ending m sound

 **Sun ends with the n sound.**

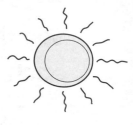

sun

Circle the pictures whose names end with the n sound.

  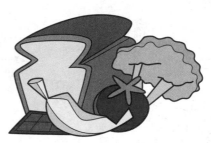 

Say the name of each picture. If it ends with the n sound, write n on the line.

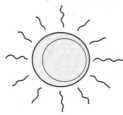   **10**

_____ _____ _____ _____

Write the ending letter to complete each word.

 i____

 fi____

  ma____

 ta____

Maze Magic

Find your way through the maze! Connect the pictures whose names end with n.

Which pictures did you connect in the maze? Circle the words that name those pictures.

pin   fin   moon   in   tan

Left or Right?

Say the name of each picture. If the word begins with the n sound, write n on the left line. If it ends with the n sound, write n on the right line.

Keep Track!

Say the name of each picture in the race track. Count how many words begin with **n** and how many end with **n**. Write the numbers below. The higher number wins the race!

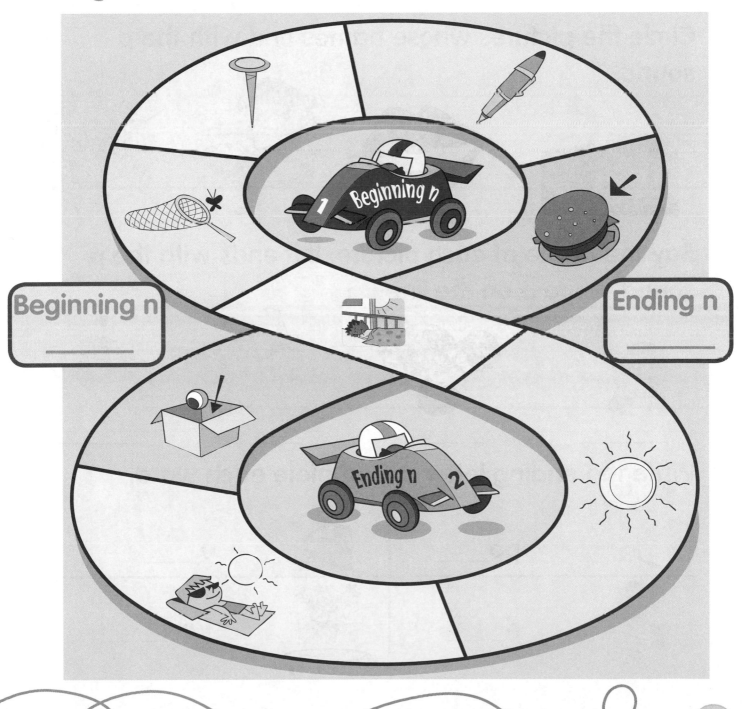

Beginning n
_____

Ending n
_____

Pp

Lip ends with the p sound.

lip

Circle the pictures whose names end with the p sound.

Say the name of each picture. If it ends with the p sound, write p on the line.

  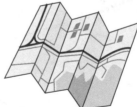 

_____   _____   _____   _____

Write the ending letter to complete each word.

 po_____ | u_____

 ri_____ |  jum_____

Hidden Picture

Say the name of each picture. If it ends with the p sound, color the space.

Look at the pictures in the spaces you colored. Circle the words that name those pictures.

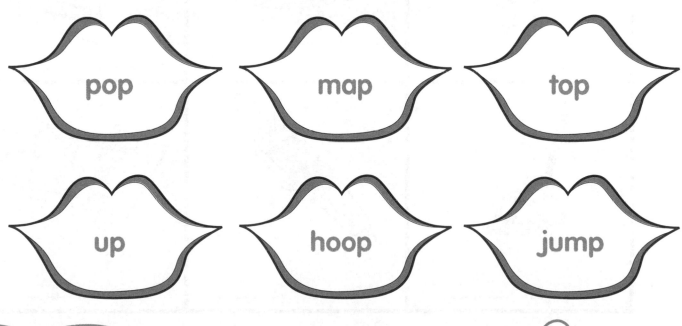

pop

map

top

up

hoop

jump

Left or Right?

Say the name of each picture. If the word begins with the **p** sound, write **p** on the left line. If it ends with the **p** sound, write **p** on the right line.

Connect Four

In each box, draw a line to connect the two pictures whose names begin with the **p** sound. Draw another line to connect those that end with the **p** sound.

Boot ends with the t sound.

boot

Circle the pictures whose names end with the t sound.

Say the name of each picture. If it ends with the t sound, write t on the line.

_____   _____   _____   _____

Write the ending letter to complete each word.

do_____    pe_____

 pi_____   hu_____

Teamwork

Circle the pictures whose names end with the **t** sound. Count the number and write it below the team. The team with the highest number wins!

Team A:

Team B:

Left or Right?

Say the name of each picture. If the word begins with the **t** sound, write **t** on the left line. If it ends with the **t** sound, write **t** on the right line.

Goal Time!

Say the name of each picture. Draw a line to connect each picture with the matching goal.

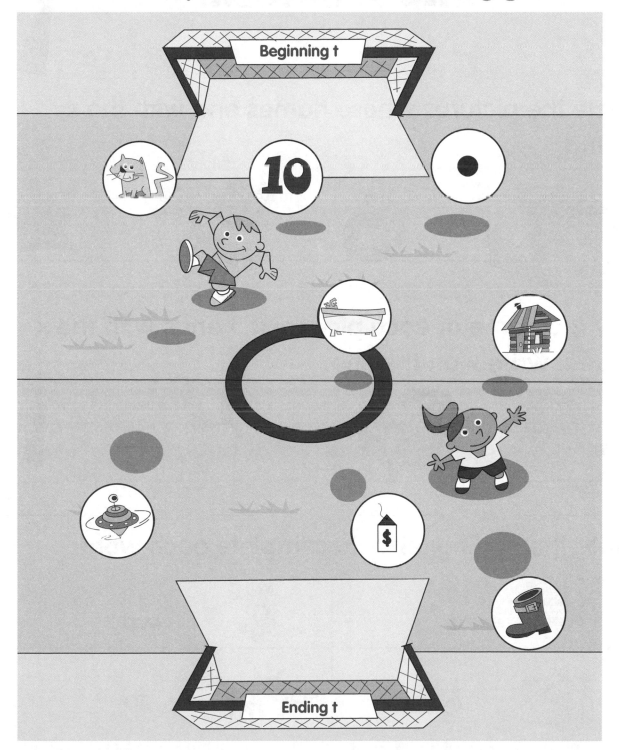

 **Ax ends with the x sound.**

ax

Circle the pictures whose names end with the x sound.

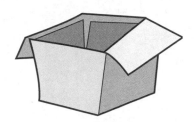  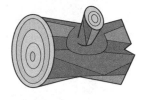

Say the name of each picture. If it ends with the x sound, write x on the line.

_____ _____ _____ _____

Write the ending letter to complete each word.

 o_____   wa_____

 fi_____    fo_____

Tic-Tac-Toe

Circle the row whose pictures all end with the x sound.

Circle the words that name the three pictures in the winning row.

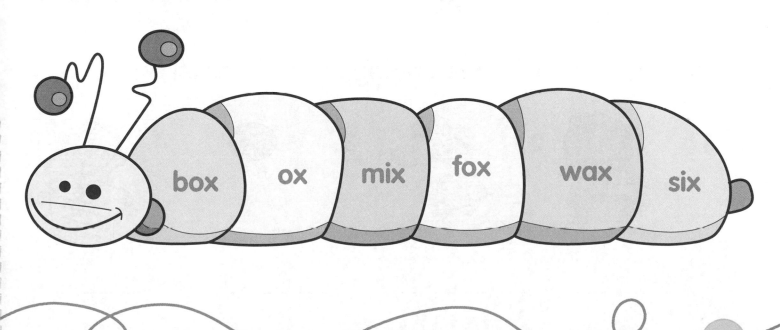

Let's Review

Say the name of the first picture in each row. Circle the pictures in the row that have the same ending sound.

Write the letter for the ending sound of each word.

1. _____   2. _____   3. _____   4. _____

Bows and Hats

Draw a line from each word to the picture it names.

moon
mom

drum
gum

fin
in

hot
top

Circle the name of each picture.

1.

mat   map

2.

sun   sum

3.

pin   pit

4.

ten   team

5.

fix   fin

6.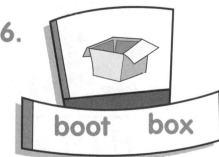

boot   box

Ff

off and **leaf** both end with the **f** sound.

off

leaf

Circle the pictures whose names end with the **f** sound.

Say the name of each picture. If it ends with the **f** sound, write **f** on the line.

_____   _____   _____   _____

Write the ending letter or letters to complete each word.

 bee_____    ree_____

 cli_____    sni_____

Hidden Picture

Say the name of each picture. If it ends with the **f** sound, color the space.

Look at the pictures in the spaces you colored. Circle the words that name those pictures.

beef

sniff

cliff

reef

off

leaf

Left or Right?

Say the name of each picture. If the word begins with the f sound, write f on the left line. If it ends with the f sound, write f on the right line.

Connect Four

In each box, draw a line to connect the two pictures whose names begin with the f sound. Draw another line to connect those that end with the f sound.

Ll

Seal and doll both end with the l sound.

doll

seal

Circle the pictures whose names end with the l sound.

  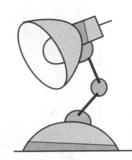 

Say the name of each picture. If it ends with the l sound, write l on the line.

_____   _____   _____   _____

Write the ending letter or letters to complete each word.

 mai____    tai____

  ta____    fa____

Maze Magic

Find your way through the maze! Connect the pictures whose names end with the **l** sound.

Which pictures did you connect in the maze? Circle the words that name those pictures.

mail   tall   bowl   doll   seal

Left or Right?

Say the name of each picture. If the word begins with the l sound, write l on the left line. If it ends with the l sound, write l on the right line.

Keep Track

Say the name of each picture in the race track. Count how many words begin with l and how many end with l. Write the numbers below. The higher number wins the race!

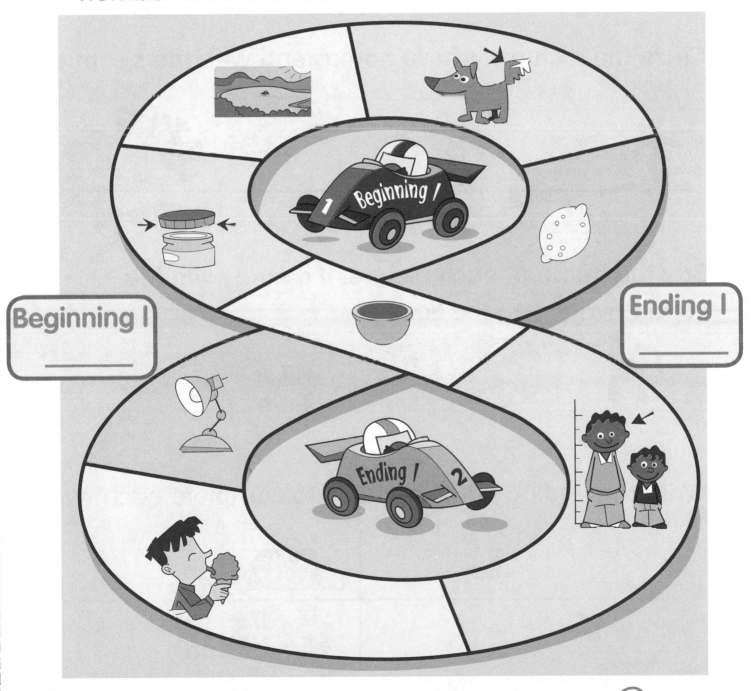

Beginning l
_____

Ending l
_____

 **Bus and dress both end with the s sound.**

dress

bus

Circle the pictures whose names end with the **s** sound.

Say the name of each picture. If it ends with the **s** sound, write **s** on the line.

 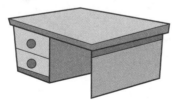  

_____   _____   _____   _____

Write the ending letter or letters to complete each word.

 gla_____

 gra_____

 to_____

 pa_____

Teamwork

Circle the pictures whose names end with the **s** sound. Count the number and write it below the team. The team with the highest number wins!

Team A:

Team B:

Left or Right?

Say the name of each picture. If the word begins with the s sound, write s on the left line. If it ends with the s sound, write s on the right line.

Goal Time!

Say the name of each picture. Draw a line to connect each picture with the matching goal.

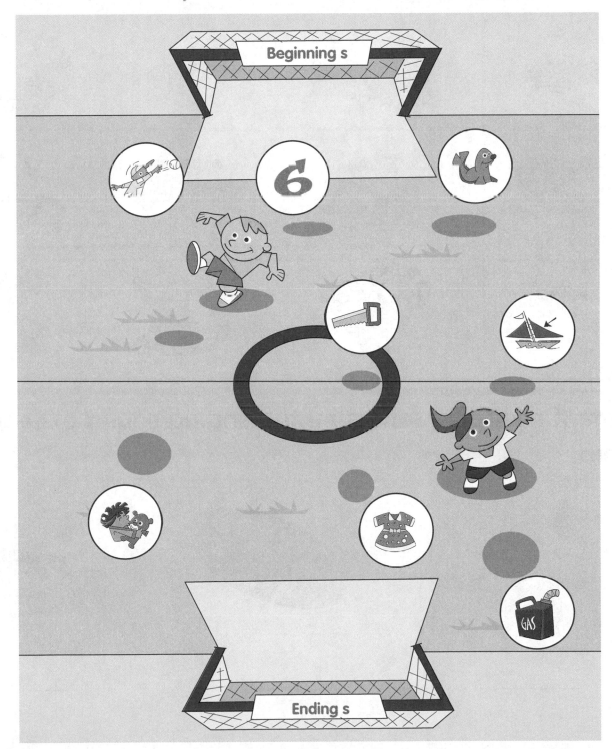

Let's Review

Say the name of the first picture in each row. Circle the pictures in the row that have the same ending sound.

1.

2.

3.

Write the letter or letters for the ending sound of each word.

1.

2.

3.

_____   _____   _____

Word Wagons

Circle the correct word for each picture.

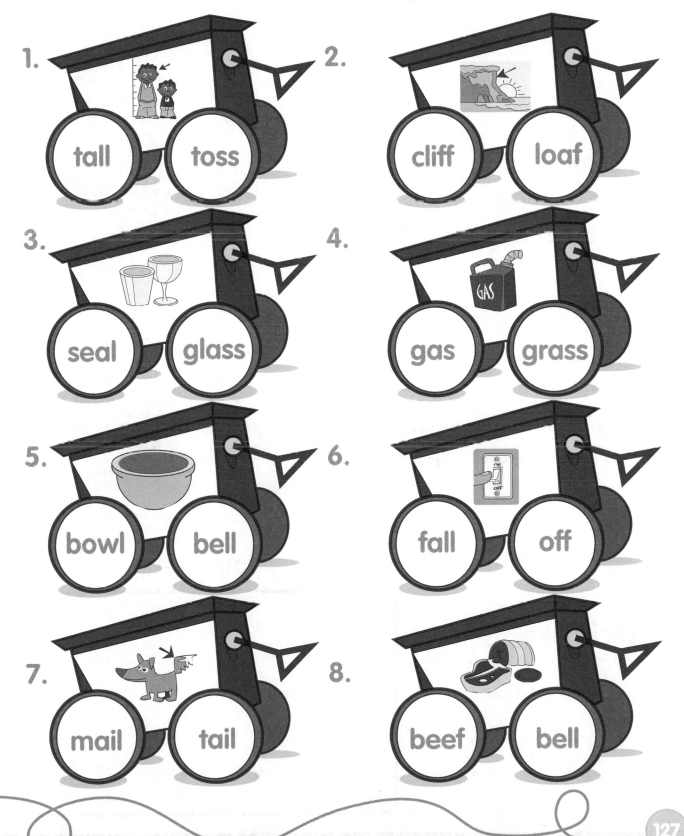

1. tall   toss

2. cliff   loaf

3. seal   glass

4. gas   grass

5. bowl   bell

6. fall   off

7. mail   tail

8. beef   bell

Picture This

Read each phrase and draw a line to the matching picture.

1. a weak man

a)

2. a tall flag

b)

3. a bowl of jam

c)

4. a box of food

d)

5. a fat fox

e)

6. a hoop in the grass

f)

Now read the phrase and draw your own picture.

six books

Read and Number

Read each sentence and find the matching picture.
Write the number by the sentence.

The maid has a pet fox. _____
Mom can cook beef. _____
I jog in the sun. _____
Toss the map in the cab. _____

Picture Search

Read the words in the box.
Find each word in the picture.
Write each word on the correct line.

top   jet   wax   crib
doll   roof   dress dad
rug   book   drum   moon

Story Time

Read the story. Write the correct word to complete each sentence.

box   seal
fin   crib
cot

1. I have a pet _____.

2. Look at his _____ and tail.

3. The _____ is too tall.

4. He's too fat for the _____.

5. The _____ will rip.

grass   tub
roof   mad
rug

6. The _____ is too weak.

7. He's in mom's _____!

8. It will leak on the _____.

9. Mom is _____.

10. The tub is on the _____, in the sun.

133

Circle the Sentence

Circle the sentence that matches the picture.

1.

a) Six girls are on the team.

b) Six girls are in a tent.

2.

a) The nut is on the cliff.

b) The hut is on the cliff.

3.

a) I fix the bus.

b) I fish the bus

4.

a) The web is on the log.

b) The wet is on the log.

Who's Who?

Read each sentence. Who does it describe? Write the name by the correct picture.

Kim can read the mail.
Tom has boots and a hood.
Sue has tan legs.
Meg has a bell on her hip.
Bob dreams about food.

2.

_____

1.
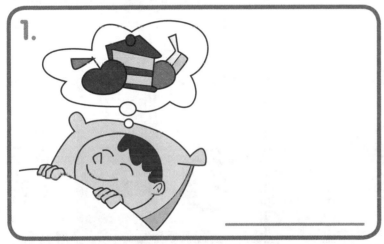
_____

3.

_____

4.

_____

5.

_____

Schoolhouse Review

Write the first and last letters to complete each word.

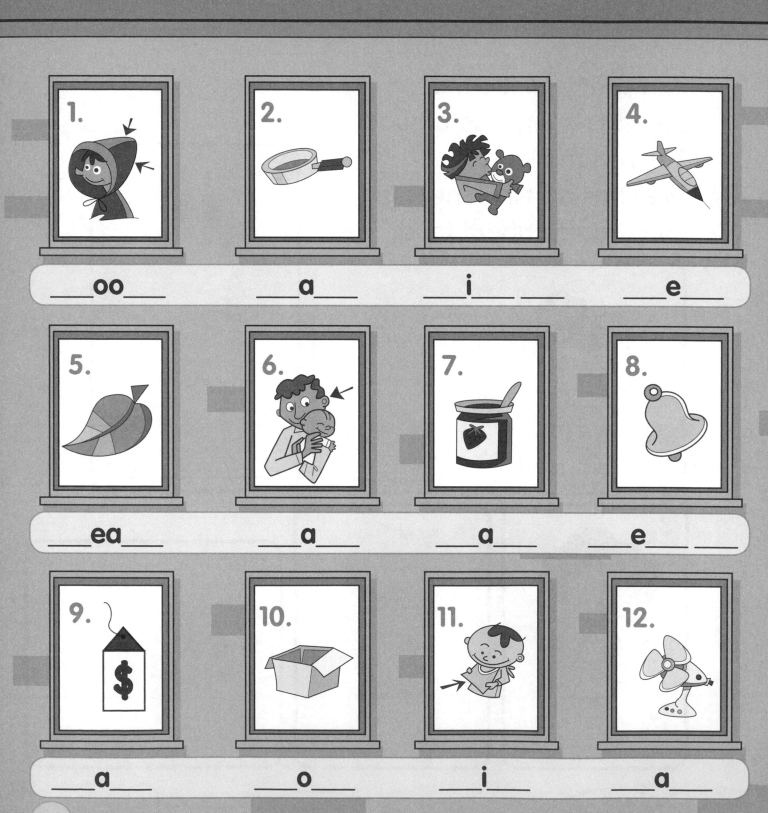

1. ___oo___

2. __a__

3. __i__ ___

4. __e__

5. ___ea__

6. __a__

7. __a__

8. __e__ _

9. __a__

10. __o__

11. __i__

12. __a__

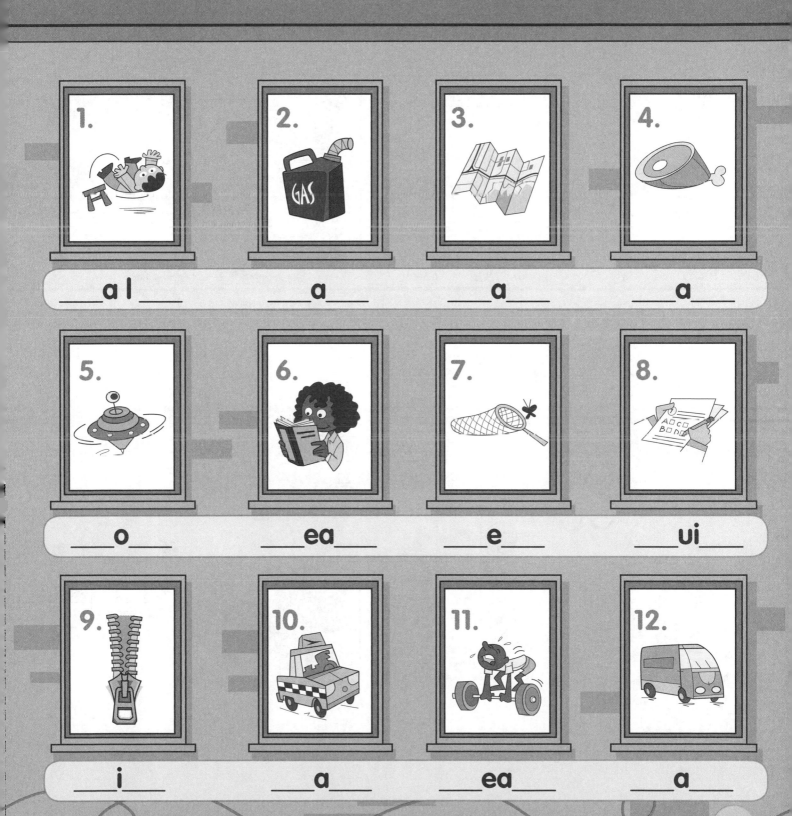

1. ___ a l ____

2. ___ a ____

3. ___ a ___

4. ___ a ___

5. ___ o ___

6. ___ ea ____

7. ___ e ___

8. ___ ui ___

9. ___ i ___

10. ___ a ___

11. ___ ea ____

12. ___ a ___

Answer Key

Page 4

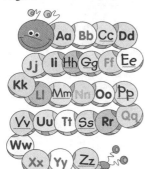

Page 5

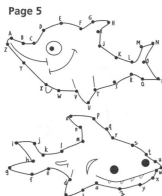

Page 6

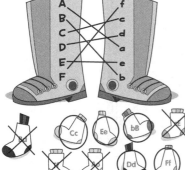

Page 7

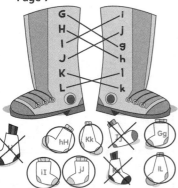

Page 8

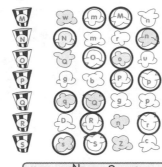

Page 9

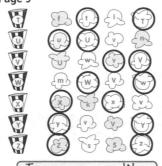

Page 10

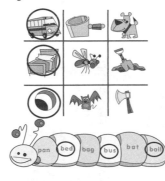

Page 11

Page 12

Page 13

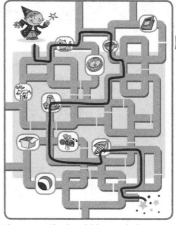

These words should be circled:
cat
car
cup
corn

Page 14

Page 15

These words should be circled:
dinner   down
dig   door

Page 16

Page 17

Team A: 4

Team B: 3

Page 18

1. dish, desk
2. bug, bus
3. face, fan
4. cup, coat

1. b   2. d   3. c   4. f

Page 19

1. dog
2. cat
3. bell
4. fish
5. fat
6. down
7. cow
8. bat

Page 20

Page 21

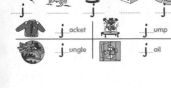
go garden game girl goat gift

Page 22

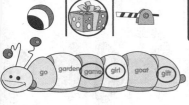

h___ h___ h___

h_at   h_ap
h_ug   h_ole

Page 23

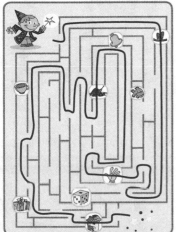

These words should be circled:
hat
hand
hay
hug

Page 24

j___   j___   j___

j_acket   j_ump
j_ungle   j_ail

Page 25

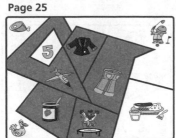

These words should be circled:
jacket   jump   jet
jeans   jam

Page 26

k___   k___   k___

k_irl   k_irk
k_itten   k_itchen

Page 27

Team A: 4

Team B: 2

Page 28

1. golf, gold
2. ketchup, king
3. juice, jump
4. hole, horse

1. h   2. g   3. k   4. j

Page 29

1. key
2. hill
3. gate
4. kitchen
5. jeep
6. juggle
7. gift
8. ham

Page 30

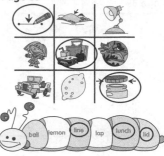

1. b
2. f
3. g
4. j
5. k
6. c
7. h
8. d

Page 31

cat / kite
dog / fog
corn / horse
bus / gas

Bottom
1. fall
2. dig
3. kiss
4. goat
5. car
6. down

Page 32

1. c
2. d
3. f
4. b
5. a
6. e

Page 33

The kangaroo can hop. 4
I put gas in the bus. 3
I juggle four cans. 1
The fish is on the dish. 2

Page 34

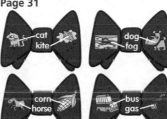

l_ap   l_ick
l_ist   l_ine

Page 35

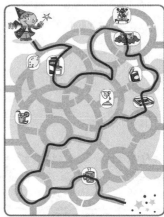
ball lemon line lap lunch lid

Page 36

m___   m___   m___

m_ad   m_ix
m_ud   m_ap

Page 37

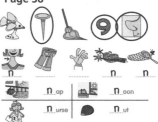

These words should be circled:
milk
mud
mat
mug

Page 38

n___ n___

n_ap   n_oon
n_urse   n_ut

139

Page 39

These words should be circled:
nose   nine
nurse   nap
nail

Page 40

p   p   p

p_in   p_ants
p_aw   p_ull

Page 41

Team A: 4

Team B: 5

Page 42

1. lick, lid
2. pot, pail
3. neck, nine
4. mop mug
1. l 2. n 3. p 4. m

Page 43

1. noon
2. lamp
3. mix
4. list
5. mouse
6. pan
7. nut
8. pin

Page 44

q_uiz   q_uiet
q_uick   q_uit

Page 45

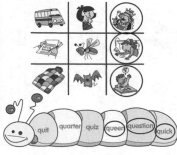

quit quarter quiz queen question quick

Page 46

r   r   r

r_ice   r_ug
r_ock   r_un

Page 47

These words should be circled:
rain
rat
ring
robot

Page 48

s_ad   s_alt
s_and   s_ing

Page 49

These words should be circled:
six   salt
soap sad
sing

Page 50

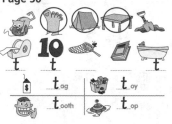

t   t   t

t_ag   t_oy
t_ooth   t_op

Page 51

Team A: 3

Team B: 2

Page 52

1. queen, quiz
2. toes, tape
3. saw, sink
4. run, rain
1. q 2. r 3. s 4. t

Page 53

1. rope
2. ring
3. sad
4. quilt
5. tag
6. rock
7. quiet
8. tent

Page 54

1. l
2. t
3. p
4. r
5. n
6. s
7. q
8. m

Page 55

1. mix
2. top
3. rose
4. queen
5. paw
6. mug

Page 56

v_egetable   v_ine
v_est   v_olleyball

Page 57

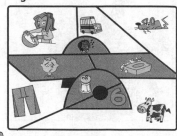

vine volcano five vest vacuum van

Page 58

W____ | W____
W____ | W____

W__arm | W__ash
W__ave | W__ind

Page 59

These words should be circled:
wagon
wet
warm
wind

Page 60

y | y

Y__ellow | Y__ell
Y__ar | Y__awn

Page 61

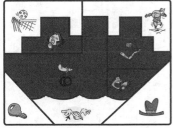

These words should be circled:
yo-yo   yarn
yell   yawn

Page 62

z | z

Z__oo | Z__ero
Z__ipper | Z__ig zag

Page 63

Team A: [2]

Team B: [3]

Page 64

1. zoo, zero
2. wagon, wash
3. yogurt, yard
4. violin, vacuum
1. z   2. y   3. w   4. v

Page 65

1. zoo
2. yell
3. yarn
4. van
5. wind
6. vine
7. window
8. zero

Page 66

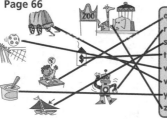

1. y
2. r
3. s
4. q
5. w
6. v
7. z
8. t

Page 67

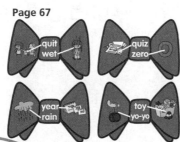

quit / wet
quiz / zero
year / rain
toy / yo-yo

1. toes
2. vine
3. zipper
4. worm
5. rat
6. table

Page 68

1. e
2. c
3. f
4. d
5. a
6. b

Page 69

I had vegetables and milk for lunch. 3
The zebra is quick. 2
A pool is in the yard. 4
We wash the van.   1

Pages 70-71

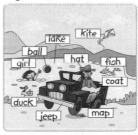

Page 72

1. Lunch is at noon.
2. The queen has vegetables.
3. The king has yams.
4. The cat has milk.
5. A bug hops.

Page 73

6. It zig zags on the table.
7. The juice falls.
8. They are sad and wet.
9. They run out the door.
10. They go in the pool.

Page 74

1. a
2. b
3. b
4. a

Page 75

1. Jill
2. Mark
3. Amy
4. Rob
5. Pete

Page 76

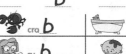

cra_b | tu_b
ru_b | bi_b

Page 77

crab web tub crib bib cub

Page 78

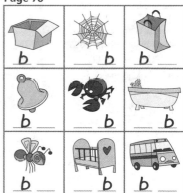

b | b | b
b | b | b
b | b | b

Page 79

Beginning b sound

Ending b sound

Page 80

rea **d** | see **d**
woo **d** | foo **d**

Page 81

These words should be circled:
maid
food
mad
dad

Page 82

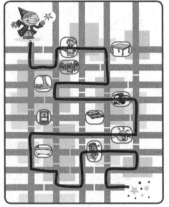

d | d | d
d | d | d
d | d | d

Page 83
Beginning d: 5
Ending d: 3

Page 84

ju **g** | ru **g**
jo **g** | ta **g**

Page 85

These words should be circled:
flag   jog   rug
wig   leg

Page 86

g | g | g
g | g | g
g | g | g

Page 87

Page 88

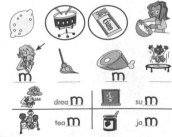

J
k | k
des **k** | loo **k**
pea **k** | wea **k**

Page 89

Team A: 4

Team B: 2

Page 90

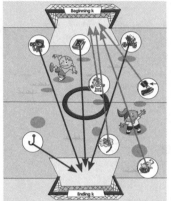

k | k | k
k | k | k
k | k | k

Page 91

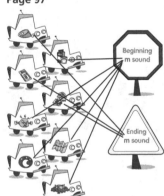

Beginning k

Ending k

Page 92
1. cook, peak
2. maid, seed
3. rub, crib
4. jug, tag
1. k   2. g   3. b   4. d

Page 93
1. rug
2. look
3. hood
4. bib
5. wood
6. crab
7. leg
8. weak

Page 94

m | m
drea **m** | su **m**
tea **m** | ja **m**

Page 95

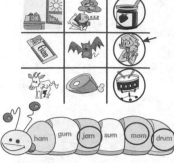

ham gum jam sum mom drum

Page 96

m | m | m
m | m | m
m | m | m

Page 97

Beginning m sound

Ending m sound

Page 98

10
n
i **n** | fi **n**
ma **n** | ta **n**

Page 99

These words should be circled:
pin
tan
in
moon

Page 100

n _____   n _____   _____ n

n   n   n

n   n   n

Page 101

Beginning n: 3
Ending n: 5

Page 102

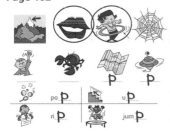

po _p_   u _p_

ri _p_   jum _p_

Page 103

These words should be circled:
pop   jump
top   hoop
up

Page 104

_p_   _p_   _p_

_p_   _p_   _p_

_p_   _p_   _p_

Page 105

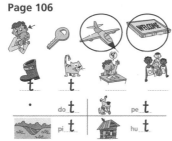

Page 106

do _t_ | pe _t_

pi _t_ | hu _t_

Page 107

Team A: 4

Team B: 3

Page 108

_t_   _t_   _t_

_t_   _t_   _t_

_t_   _t_   _t_

Page 109

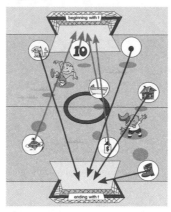

beginning with t

ending with t

Page 110

o _x_ | wa _x_

fi _x_ | fo _x_

Page 111

box   ox   mix   fox   wax   six

Page 112

1. jam, ham
2. lip, up
3. jet, dot
4. fox, ax

1. x   2. m   3. n   4. p

Page 113

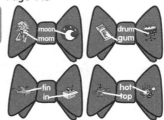

moon — mom
drum — gum
fin — in
hot — top

1. map
2. sun
3. pin
4. ten
5. fix
6. box

Page 114

bee _f_ | ree _f_

cli _ff_ | sni _ff_

Page 115

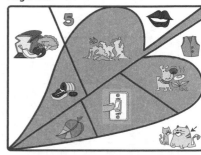

5

These words should be circled:
reef
sniff
off
beef
leaf

Page 116

_f_   _f_   _f_

_f_   _f_   _f_

_f_   _f_   _f_

Page 117

Page 118

mai_l   tai_l

ta_ll   fa_ll

Page 119

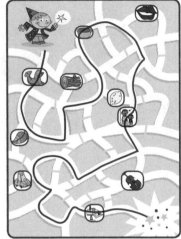

These words should be circled:

seal   bowl
tall   mail

Page 120

Page 121

Beginning l: 5
Ending l: 3

Page 122

gla_SS   gro_SS

to_SS   pa_SS

Page 123

Team A: 3

Team B: 5

Page 124

S   S   S

S   S   S

S   S   S

Page 125

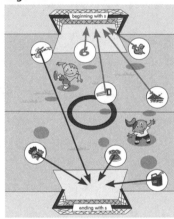

Page 126

1. bell, seal
2. sniff, roof
3. kiss, dress
1. l   2. f   3. s

Page 127

1. tall
2. cliff
3. glass
4. gas
5. bowl
6. off
7. tail
8. beef

Page 128

1. d
2. e
3. f
4. a
5. c
6. b

Page 129

The maid has a pet fox. 2
Mom can cook beef. 3
I jog in the sun. 1
Toss the map in the cab. 4

Pages 130

Page 131

Page 132

1. I have a pet seal.
2. Look at his fin and tail.
3. The crib is too tall.
4. He's too fat for the box.
5. The cot will rip.

Page 133

6. The roof is too weak.
7. He's in mom's tub.
8. It will leak on the rug.
9. Mom is mad.
10. The tub is on the grass, in the sun.

Page 134

1. a
2. b
3. a
4. a

Page 135

1. Bob
2. Kim
3. Meg
4. Tom
5. Sue

Page 136

1. hood
2. pan
3. kiss
4. jet
5. leaf
6. dad
7. jam
8. bell
9. tag
10. box
11. bib
12. fan

Page 137

1. fall
2. gas
3. map
4. ham
5. top
6. read
7. net
8. quiz
9. zip
10. cab
11. weak
12. van

OTHER BOOKS TO LOOK FOR

**The Classic paper Costumes of Dong
Theatre,** R. D. McAllister
Art Dicko, M. O'Connor
The Nippon Slipon: Adornment for the
New Age, Dr Itazura
Cozzies for Aussies: Dressing Up Down
Under, P. Camp

VISIT THE KOKIGAMI WEB SITE

http://www.kokigami.com

Now you can join the Kokigami on-line
community and discover what others are
doing with their kokis all round the world.

Performance Enhancing Adornments for the Adventurous Man **KOKIGAMI -**

KOKIGAMI

Performance Enhancing

Adornments for the Adventurous Man

TEN SPEED PRESS

Berkeley/Toronto

*"Every creative act involves...a new innocence of perception,
liberated from the catarat of accepted belief."- Arthur Koestler.*

Ten Speed Press
P.O.Box 7123
Berkeley, California 94707
www.tenspeed.com

Distributed in Australia by Simon and Schuster Australia, in Canada
by Ten Speed Press Canada, in New Zealand by Southern Publishers
Group, in South Africa by Real Books, in Southeast Asia by Berkeley
Books, and in United Kingdom and Europe by Airlift Book
Company.

Grateful thanks to the trustees for access to the O'Connor Main
Collection.

Design by Trevor Plaisted
Cover photograph by Annelies Vanderpoel.

Library of Congress Cataloging-in-Publication Data is on file with
the publisher.

ISBN 1-58008-245-9

This book is intended for entertainment and humor purposes only.
Neither the artist, author, nor the publishers will assume
responsibility for the use or misuse of any information or artwork
contained within this book.

First printing, 2000
Printed in Hong Kong

www.kokigami.com

1 2 3 4 5 6 7 8 9 10 - 05 04 03 02 01 00

CONTENTS

■

Foreword ——————————————————————————— 8

An Historical Perspective ————————————————— 10

Getting Started ———————————————————————— 12

Instructions ————————————————————————— 15

Sizing ———————————————————————————— 17

The Dragon ———————————————————————— 18

The Cock —————————————————————————— 23

The Squid ———————————————————————— 24

The Moth ——————————————————————————— 29

The Pig ——————————————————————————— 30

The Fish ————————————————————————— 37

The Horse —————————————————————————— 38

The Dog ——————————————————————————— 43

The Rose ——————————————————————————— 44

The Car ——————————————————————————— 49

The Steam Engine —————————————————————— 50

The Space Shuttle —————————————————————— 57

The Fire Engine ——————————————————————— 58

The Private Investigator ——————————————————— 63

Biographical Notes ————————————————————— 64

F OREWORD

■

okigami has fascinated me since 1974 when I was introduced to it by the delightful Dr. Itazura in Tokyo. One afternoon while discussing male sexual awareness in our respective cultures, Dr. Itazura mentioned that the art of the little paper costume was clear evidence of the Japanese male's ability to gain a deeper intellectual and emotional understanding of his libidinal urges. Naturally I asked him what this art was. Without replying he stood up and left the room, returning a moment later with an ornately carved sandalwood box which he carefully placed on the floor in front of me. Inside were a collection of colorful paper sculptures that looked for all the world like children's toys or Christmas tree decorations. When I suggested that this was what they were, he laughed and fetched a series of old scrolls which clearly showed just how wrong I was.

I had of course heard of the Nippon Slip-on and for that matter I was familiar with the expression Art Dicko, but had, like many other Westerners, assumed that these terms referred to the colorful and often ornate condoms favored by Japanese of high breeding. As a sexologist I prided myself with my knowledge of things erotic, but here before me was hard evidence of a most advanced sexual practice that clearly left the likes of the Karma Sutra for dead. This was not some sex manual that promoted a variety of interesting physical positions, but a most ingenious

method of heightening the enjoyment of the sex act by putting the participants in touch with their inner sexual fantasies. What could be more intriguing!

For the Japanese, the pleasures of the flesh are natural and normal, and sexual happiness has always been regarded as a basic human right. Given these attitudes and the advanced nature of their culture, it is not surprising that they developed a highly sophisticated method of increasing sexual enjoyment.

The male has always been dominant in Japanese society and from the earliest times ensured that his sexual needs were well catered by the availability of women trained in the art of lovemaking. Having taken this training to an extremely high level it was obvious to him, as it seems not to have been to other cultures, that any additional pleasure could only be found by somehow training his own sexual ability, the center of which was the phallus. This I believe was the guiding principle behind the evolution of Kokigami.

This beautifully simple system allows the mind to get more deeply in touch with the male sexual center by pretending that it is something else. By slipping a paper sculpture of an animal over his organ, the male is able to give it the qualities of that animal and relate to it on another level. It instantly becomes far more than a rather odd piece of blood-engorged flesh with a mind of its own. It is given a new personality, making the organ much easier to relate to and therefore to understand and control.

More importantly perhaps for us in the West is that Kokigami enables women to come to terms with the male organ and relate to it in a nonthreatening way. In a practice spanning more than thirty years I have found no better method of quickly demystifying the penis and dispelling its perceived power; no other simple technique that enables couples to overcome their inhibitions, get in touch with their guiding fantasies, and so move to more loving, understanding, and pleasurable sexual relations.

But you mustn't get the idea that Kokigami is all terribly serious and something that only sex therapists should use. On the contrary, its wonderfully simple techniques are based upon having a great deal of light-hearted fun, designed to relax and encourage intimacy.

Indeed the only problem with this art form is that Western males find it initially very difficult to accept. Unlike the more sensitive Japanese, his attitudes toward sex are almost exclusively physically based, so the notion of slipping something over his member that does not have some immediate physical function, like a condom, is totally foreign to him. This fixation with his physical sexuality renders him incapable of fully understanding his complete sensual self. At best he gets only half the picture, and finding it incomprehensible, begins to build up negative feelings. Sadly, these feelings lead to much of the frustration and violence which typifies many Western relationships. It is my firm belief that Kokigami can do a great deal to restore the much needed balance between the mental and physical, and I am sure this first introduction to this art form will go a long way towards achieving that.

There are no special tricks to this art of the little paper costume. No hours of practice, no tedious new vocabulary to learn. With this book and a pair of scissors, you can add a whole new dimension to your own and your partner's sexuality. Once you get past the absurd taboos that inhibit sexual expression and understanding in our society, you'll be able to use Kokigami to bring a new meaning and pleasure to your sensual world.

Dr. Mary Scrott

Dr. Mary Scrott

INTRODUCTION

The origins of Kokigami have traditionally been the subject of spirited academic debate. On the one side are those who claim it has direct links with *origami*, the art of paper folding, while on the other are those who consider it owes its genesis to *kirigami*, or cut art. It seems likely however that it predated both of these paper art forms, as erotic prints (*shunga*) clearly show the little paper costume in use as early as the eighth century. In recent times there seems to be a general consensus amongst Oriental and Western scholars alike that kokigami probably evolved from the ancient Japanese art of *Tsutsumi* or packaging.

The word Tsutsumi comes from the verb Tsutsushimu, to refrain, to be discreet or moderate. The Japanese culture shuns the direct, the frank or blunt in favor of things which are indirect, controlled, and restrained. This ethic plays an important role in gift giving, where it is considered most discourteous to pass an unwrapped, unconcealed gift to another.

It was natural that in male-dominated Japanese society the gift that was perceived to be the most important of all, the giver of life, would be treated in the same manner. Indeed there is clear evidence from early literature that men of the upper classes wrapped their penises before retiring to the conjugal chamber. Several passages in the *Kojiki*, a book of legends dating from A.D. 712,

tell of men spending "much time with fine silks and ribbons." For the more complex he could make the wrapping, the longer his wife would take to unwrap "the present" and the more he would be rewarded by "the pleasure of the fingers undoing."

The Japanese love of ceremony formalized these "gift giving" sessions and infused them with a degree of restrained elegance which would be of great interest to us today had the practice continued. The reasons why it ceased completely are unclear, but there can be no doubt it was the forerunner of Kokigami as we know it today.

The switch in emphasis from the purely physical pleasures enjoyed in the old tsutsumi ceremony to a concentration on heightened satisfaction through mental control, as practiced in Kokigami, came about with the arrival of Buddhism in the sixth century. The deeply held Shinto beliefs in the divinity of the phallus were not wiped out by Buddhism, but rather absorbed by it, and modified. It seems likely that many aspects of Kokigami as it was practiced from the eighth century on were developed by Shinto priests. Strongly influenced by Buddhism, they sought ways of transcending the physical center of their being by exploring it in greater depth, trying to get in touch with it in much the same way an actor gets in touch with his character.

Indeed the similarity of these methods and those used in Japanese noh theater are often noted when reference is made to the derivation of the word Kokigami. *Gami* is the word for paper, and a *koki* is a small piece of cloth worn at the waist by the supporting actors (*waki*) in noh theater. All the actors in noh are male, and they use the koki in a variety of ways to make quick character changes. It can be used as a hat, a blindfold, a mask, even a weapon. While it is highly unlikely that koki were ever used to cover the male organ during a performance, their function as dramatic changers of character fits well with the concepts of Kokigami.

By the middle of the Heian period (794-1185), Japan's great golden era of artistic development, Kokigami had become firmly established as a path to sensual enlightenment amongst the aristocratic classes. But it was not until the late eighteenth century, when the price of paper fell, that it ceased to be the exclusive preserve of the rich and became popular with all strata of Japanese society. In recent years Kokigami has attracted a lot of interest from psychotherapists in America and it seems likely that this ancient art will soon enjoy a new popularity in the West.

The Goose was a popular koki in eighteenth-century Japan.

GETTING STARTED

遊び好きなお魚ちゃんがまた碧汁目に入りたがっているわ
イカはイカで感じやすい足を悶えてやっと見つけた獲物を
逃すまいと必死でがんばっているの

"Lovers at Play" from an early nineteenth-century print.

Most Western men react to Kokigami with a mixture of disbelief, embarrassment, and indignation. Surely no male would consider twirling about in front of his lover with a paper fish slipped over his most intimate organ. And making cheeky bubble sounds through protruding lips at the same time? You can't be serious! It's a natural reaction that rises mainly from a lack of knowledge about the gentle and restrained way in which this ancient art is approached.

In Japan, Kokigami is practiced with a great deal of subtlety and refinement that minimizes any initial social discomfort. While some men may feel relaxed about wearing a koki straight away, most will benefit from the more oblique traditional methods of introduction, which are based on a delightful blend of intimacy, surprise, and humor.

A good way of getting started is to gift wrap the book and hide it under your partner's pillow. This will enable you to share it together in an intimate and supportive setting. Study the pictures carefully and ask each other which you most like and dislike. Which koki do you think would be most appropriate for him to wear? Which ones can you imagine your friends or your father wearing? When making your choice of which koki to begin with, don't forget that the partner will be required to play a complimentary character. For many couples these first discussions can be most revealing and quickly lead to a deeper understanding of one's own and each other's unique erotic personalities.

Under each picture you will find the script, or *serifu*, which is divided up into the Character, the Call, the Reply, and the Play. While they are only

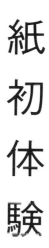

intended as suggestions, reading them out to each other should help you to clarify your feelings about them and get you in the mood to start. You will notice that the serifu, in most cases translated directly from the Japanese, are rich with sexual imagery and the double entendre. This is quite traditional and is done in order to provoke discussion and provide a certain degree of levity which relaxes the participants.

However, they are only intended as a guide to get you started and need not be followed to the letter. Indeed, it has always been assumed that couples will make up their own, much longer dialogues, into which they can weave information of a more personal nature.

Now is a good time to discuss what will happen in your Play. What will you say and do, and how will it end? Remember, innovation is the key with Kokigami. The more avenues that can be explored, the more barriers will be broken down, and the more pleasures that can be enjoyed.

Before cutting out the first koki, it's a good idea to help your partner check his size, using the sizing diagram, or *kata*, on page 17. Many men in the West are sensitive about their size, so he may be a little reluctant at first to reveal his dimensions. If your man is small in that department it's important to reassure him by downplaying the

importance of size. It may also help to point out that with Kokigami you are only interested in the width and not the length.

Once you have made your koki it's important that it be presented subtly before actually being worn. In Japan, koki were traditionally placed so as to just peep suggestively out of the little drawer at the bottom of the pillow box. Nowadays nobody uses pillow boxes, and koki are placed in an intriguing variety of places designed to surprise and excite: on the bedroom door handle, as part of an ikebana arrangement (see back cover), in a little nest made out of sheet folds — the possibilities are endless. But remember, the position you choose should be appropriate to the character of the koki. For example you might hide the Dragon in a cave of bedclothes and let your partner find it with a flashlight.

In order to help overcome any initial embarrassment that may be felt when wearing a koki, it is helpful to begin with a very low light. (The use of candles while wearing paper koki is not advisable). Music, too, is useful in setting a relaxed mood and, if in character with the koki, will greatly enhance the experience. You may like to play the sound track from a TV series like "The Untouchables" or "Naked City" when wearing the Private Investigator. "The Yellow Rose of Texas" would go well with the Rose, "Fly Me To The Moon" for the Space Shuttle, "Chattanooga Choo Choo" with the Steam Engine, and Peter, Paul, and Mary's "Car, Car" or "Puff the Magic Dragon" are just a few examples of songs that could provide the right atmosphere and give him something to move in time with.

Some men like to put their koki on themselves and surprise their lovers, but many find their partner's involvement in this delicate stage helps overcome any initial awkwardness. Touch and stroke the koki as if it were real. Talk and sing to it, play with it, become totally familiar with it before you slip it on, and once it is on, keep up the dialogue.

In order to explore the deep character of each koki the Japanese do a very effective exercise called *Renso Gehmu*, which you may like to try. The koki is put on without the partner looking and covered with a little cloth or tissue. The wearer then makes noises and movements appropriate to his character while his partner tries to guess which one he is wearing. (With over six hundred different koki currently available in Japan, this can be a daunting task.) In order to keep his partner from guessing, the wearer adopts the most subtle, minimalist forms of character expression.

Many couples enjoy personalizing their koki by decorating them with things like wool, feathers, leaves, sequins, or glitter, and they often spray them with their favorite perfumes. Luminous paint is also well worth a try. It makes for a most exciting display with all the lights turned off.

As Kokigami becomes a regular part of your sexual lifestyle, you will find new areas of exploration occur quite naturally. Trying unusual settings, working at co-operative and multi-koki wearing, and experiencing the interesting complexities of advanced group play are just a few of the delights that await you on your journey into the inner depths of your sensual self.

INSTRUCTIONS

■ *A n d   S i z i n g*

ead all the instructions through carefully before you start. You will need a sharp pair of scissors for cutting the outside edge, a sharp blade for making the slots and for fine cutting, round pencil or pen for stretching the paper, plus nimble fingers and lots of time and desire.

Cutting and Construction:

Remember to check your personal size by using the sizing diagram on page 17 before you begin. This will ensure a firm and comfortable fit. Only cut the slits that relate to your size so as not to weaken the tabs with too many cuts.

When cutting, follow the solid black lines around the edge of each piece of the pattern. Black lines also indicate slots which will need to be cut with the blade. Take care to find all the slots as there are usually quite a few and they are sometimes hard to find. They all need to be cut out on a flat surface before the construction process begins.

Dotted lines indicate folds, and you will need to check whether they should be made into a hill or a valley. You can do this by referring to the picture of the completed koki.

Folding:

Special folding is sometimes necessary to give extra rigidity and strength. The most dramatic example of this is the Fire Engine's long extension ladder. To make it stiff and strong, the edge of the ladder is folded. The running board along the edge of the Fire Engine also uses this technique, as do the other vehicles, to hold its shape.

Stretching:

This process is used to twist or curl the paper. Using the side of a pencil, pull the paper firmly between your thumb and the pencil. Repeat until the paper falls into a natural curl. Take care not to pull too hard and rip the paper. This technique is used in shaping the Squid's tentacles, the fringe of the Horse, the tail feathers of the Cock, and to a lesser extent on the Moth's and Dragon's feelers. It is also used to shape the front bumper of the Sports Car, the feelers of the Fish, the hairy tips of the Pig's ears and the Dog's ears.

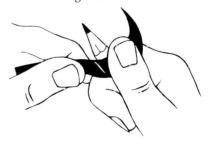

Interlocking:

The koki are held together by means of tags and slots. No glue or tape is normally required, though some taping may be advisable after frequent vigorous use.

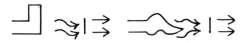

These tags have to be eased and wriggled in sideways, then straightened in line with the slot.

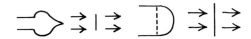

These are less secure so once through they should be bent over.

These tags are very secure. They are folded small to fit through the slot, then unfolded once in place.

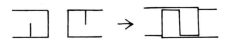

These lock together, slot to slot, and lie flat to form one continuous band. They are mostly used to attach the koki to the penis.

Construction:

Once it is cut, folded, and stretched, construct the koki by following the alphabet. For example, A goes to A1, then A2 goes to A3, and so on, depending on how many steps are needed to attach and position each piece of the pattern. The next piece will be B, which will go to B1 and so on.

Order of Difficulty:

Like origami, Kokigami is a very old paper art that has been refined over the centuries to enable its practice with a minimum of skill. Even so, it is a good idea to begin with the easiest patterns first. The most basic ones are the Moth and then the Rose. The Dog, Squid, Private Investigator, Fire Engine, Dragon, Fish, and Sports Car are a little more difficult. The most advanced are the Cock, Horse, Space Shuttle, Pig, and lastly the Steam Engine.

DOG: LEAD ATTACHMENT.

FIRE ENGINE: ATTACHING THE EXTENSION LADDER.

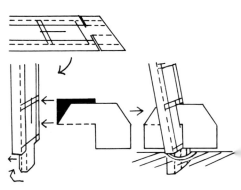

COCK: SHAPING THE BEAK.

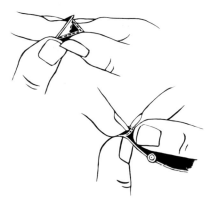

How to Measure Your Size

It is important to take care with the sizing to ensure your koki fits firmly and doesn't fall off during The Play. This can be embarrassing and inhibit the natural flow of action and dialogue.

When sizing, the organ should be rigid and pressed down firmly onto this page. As this creates a rather difficult viewing angle, it is a good idea to get your partner to check your reading.

Measure the size at the thickest part (usually the stem) by looking down directly over the top of the organ or by using a flat surface laid along its side. Having found your width (e.g., B+, C, etc), you can cut out the two corresponding slits marked on the holding tabs and be assured of a good fit. Remember to cut only the slits for your size so as not to weaken the tabs with too many cuts.

A   B   C

A+   B+
B−   C−

Sizing

RYU : THE DRAGON

The crafty Dragon likes to breathe his fire into the dark jeweled cave. Ravaging, vengeful, sly.

THE CALL: *"Where are my precious jewels? My treasures? My trophies? Are they hidden there in your dark cave?"*

THE REPLY: *"Come on hot stuff! Careful the iron gates don't snap shut and sever your burning tongue!"*

THE PLAY: *With arms outstretched and fingers curled like claws, move forward warily with the knees bent. The hips may be flicked about spasmodically accompanied by the low seductive roar of a raging furnace.*

19

22

へざあ　ばあとん

ONDORI : THE COCK

台詞

The haughty cock puffs himself up and crows arrogantly from the roof top. Inflated, vain, jubilant.

THE CALL: *"Cock-a-doodle-doo!"*
THE REPLY: *"Get lost feather brain!"*
THE PLAY: *Strut about stiffly with hands on hips and the head held high. Crow loudly infront of your partner, but then move closer and make exciting little clucking sounds.*

23

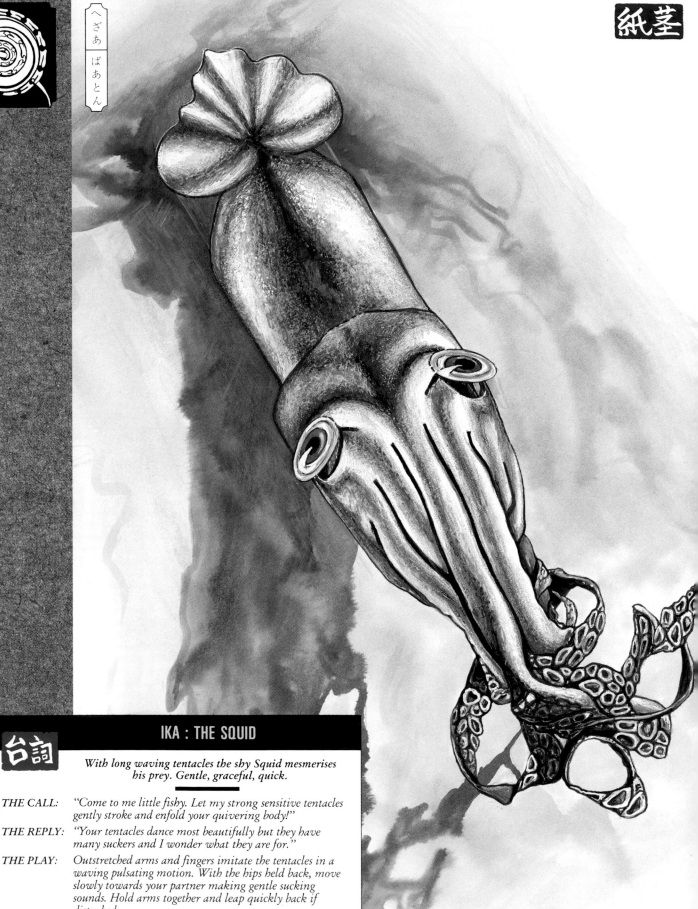

Ika

紙茎

へ ざ あ
ば あ と ん

台詞

IKA : THE SQUID

With long waving tentacles the shy Squid mesmerises his prey. Gentle, graceful, quick.

———

THE CALL: *"Come to me little fishy. Let my strong sensitive tentacles gently stroke and enfold your quivering body!"*

THE REPLY: *"Your tentacles dance most beautifully but they have many suckers and I wonder what they are for."*

THE PLAY: Outstretched arms and fingers imitate the tentacles in a waving pulsating motion. With the hips held back, move slowly towards your partner making gentle sucking sounds. Hold arms together and leap quickly back if disturbed.

28

へ ざ あ ば あ と ん

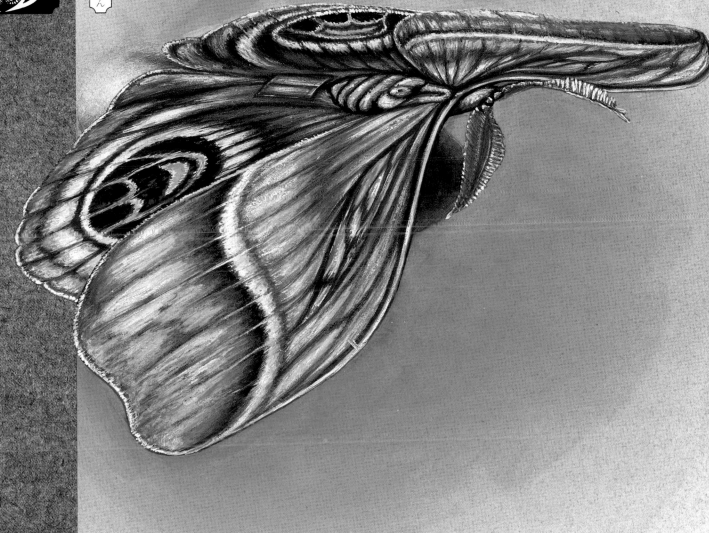

GA : THE MOTH

Fluttering silently on silken wings the Moth is hopelessly intoxicated by the light. Soft, vulnerable, tender.

THE CALL: *"I am dazzled by your brightness. Let me bathe in the glow of your sparkling radiance."*

THE REPLY: *"Hotter and hotter burns my glistening light! Beware you do not singe your beautiful silken wings."*

THE PLAY: *Stand on tiptoes and take precise little steps, twirling around your partner with arms and fingers fluttering in a wing-like manner. Allow the lips, head, and hips to tremble slightly.*

BUTA : THE PIG

The happy Pig likes to root about in the soft earth with his pink nose. Eager, expectant, watchful.

———

THE CALL: *"Oink! Oink! How about a bit of juicy swill?"*

THE REPLY: *"Here Piggy Wiggy! Lots of lovely warm slops just for you!"*

THE PLAY: *Thrust the hips forward and up with short jerky movements while jumping quickly towards your partner. Make low, enticing grunts. If thwarted, jump back and emit a startled squeal.*

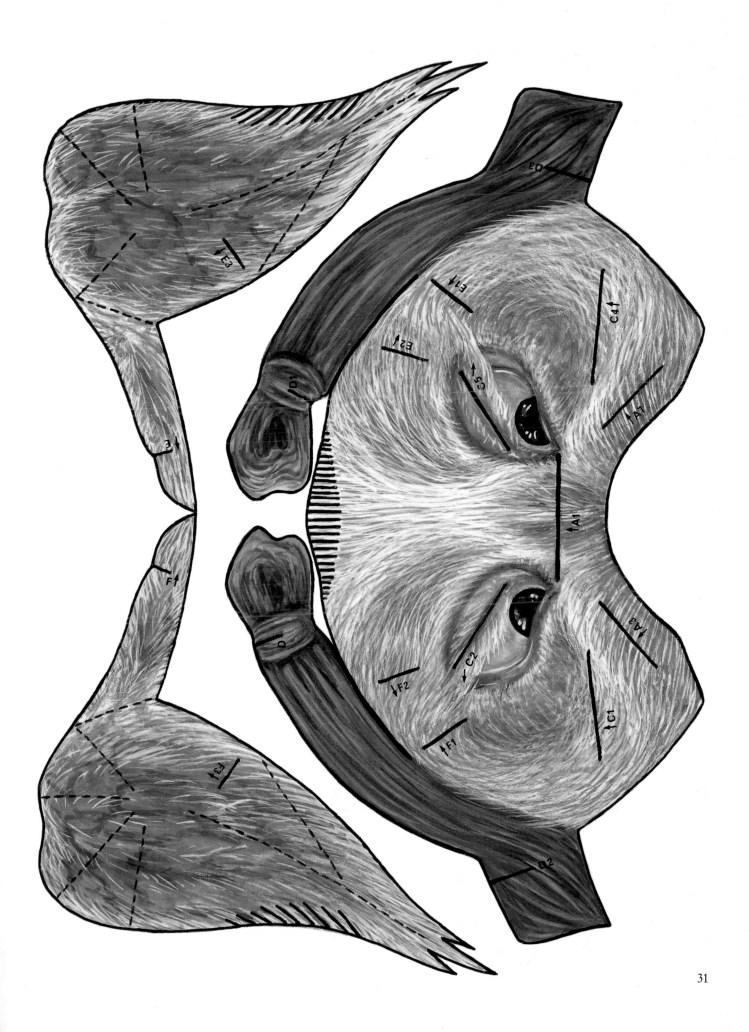

31

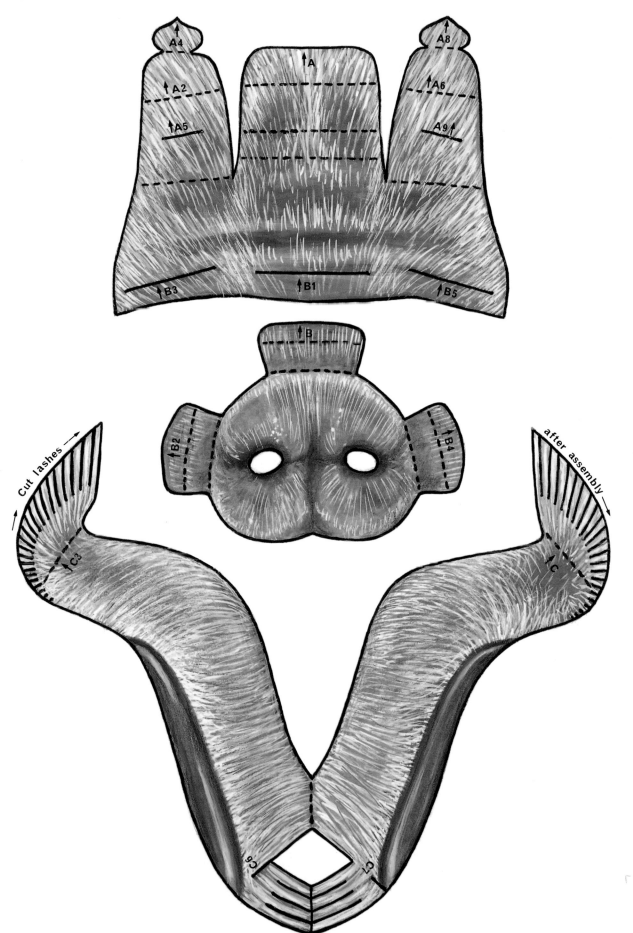

33

Sakana

紙茎

へざあ　ばあとん

SAKANA : THE FISH

*The playful Fish likes to wriggle through the weeds
and dart into crevices. Fun-loving, alert, sleek.*

THE CALL: *"Hey little sea anemone, your tiny red tentacles can't
catch me!"*

THE REPLY: *"Can't they just! Let's wait and see!"*

THE PLAY: *With arms held out from the body to simulate fins, dart
enticingly about in front of your partner making cheeky
bubble sounds through protruding lips.*

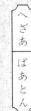

UMA : THE HORSE

With flared nostrils and flowing mane the mighty Horse gallops into the forest. Strong, noble, free.

THE CALL: *"Where are my oats? Where is my straw?"*

THE REPLY: *"Your oats are ready, the straw is warm and my stable door is open, but you still have a long way to go!"*

THE PLAY: *With reins held firmly in both hands, raise the knees high and gallop towards your partner. The rider may call out, "Whoa! Easy boy!" and pull back on the reins while at the same time thrusting the hips forward violently.*

39

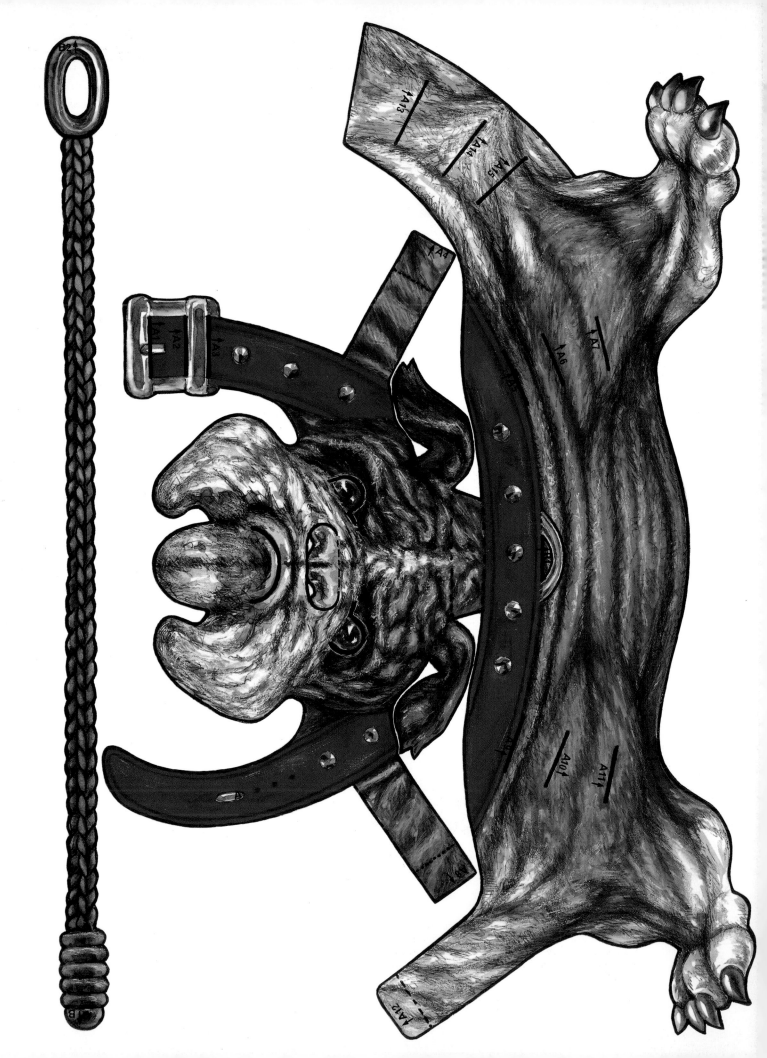

Inu

INU : THE DOG

The muscle-bound Dog strains at his leash pulling his master off balance. Slobbery, powerful, disobedient.

THE CALL: "Ruff! Ruff! Let me get at that pussy cat!"

THE REPLY: "Meow!"

THE PLAY: One hand grasps the leash attempting to restrain the dog while at the same time the hips are thrust vigorously forward and back to simulate his attempts at freedom. The master may shout, "Sit!" "Lie down!" or "Get in behind!"

43

紙茎

へ ざ あ
ば あ と ん

台詞

BARA : THE ROSE

In full bloom, the delicate Rose unfolds its velvet petals.
Fragrance abounds. Vibrant, aromatic, thorny.

THE CALL: *"Come fuzzy bee and taste my pearly nectar! Feel my soft*
petals against your tiny cheeks!"

THE REPLY: *"Buzzzzz, hold still sweet-scented beauty and let my long*
tongue probe your honey hole."

THE PLAY: *The feet are held together and the body stretched upwards*
like the main stem. Then the forearms are extended out
like other stems and the hands become more blooms
quivering seductively in the breeze.

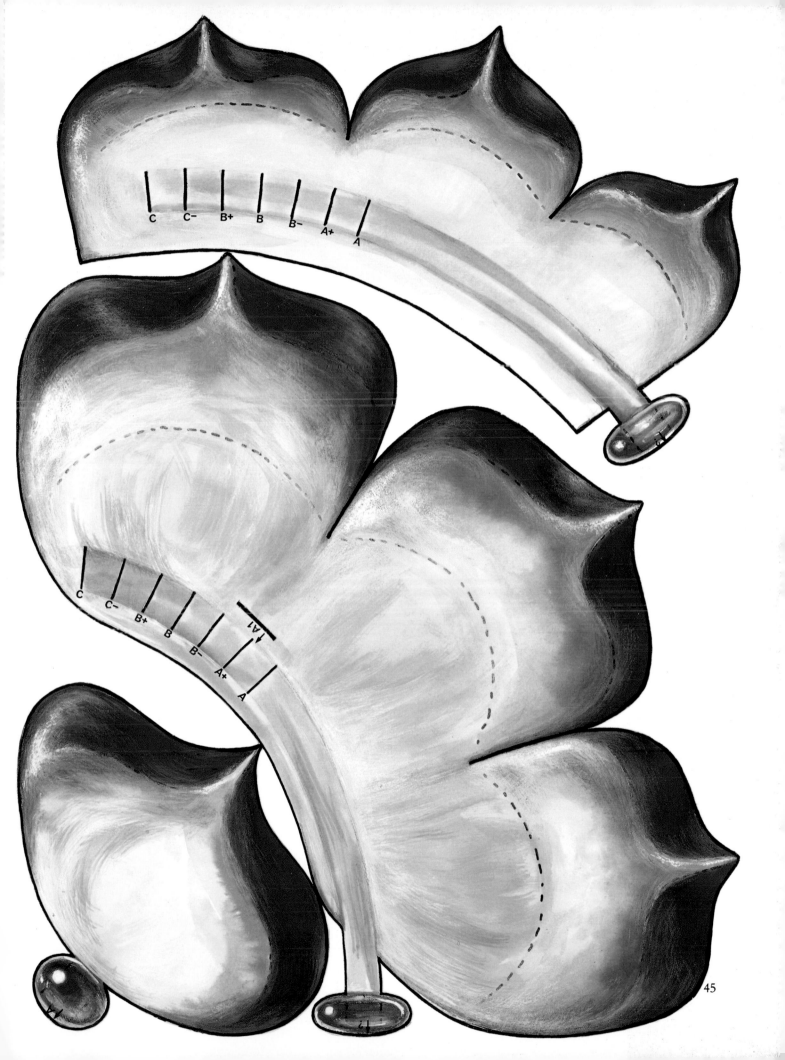

Kuruma

紙茎

へ ざ あ
ば あ と ん

台詞

KURUMA : THE SPORTS CAR

*The Sports Car speeds along narrow country lanes,
squealing noisily as it accelerates round corners. Fast,
exciting, flashy.*

THE CALL: *"Rrrrrrrmmmmm! Beep! Beep! Hey can you give me a
hand to park this thing?"*

THE REPLY: *Left hand down a bit, bit more.....Plenty of room on this
side....Steady....Whoa! That's far enough!"*

THE PLAY: *One hand is held in front gripping the steering wheel
while the other changes gear. The hips are thrust forward
and the shoulders back, make deep throbbing exhaust
noises.*

へざあ　ばあとん

KISHA : THE STEAM ENGINE

With smoke belching and cinders flying the big Steam Engine roars out of the tunnel. Proud, throbbing, hot.

THE CALL:　*"Chuff chuff chuff chuff, chuff chuff chuff chuff, Whooooooooooooooooo! Got to make it! Got to make it!"*

THE REPLY:　*"Please stand well clear of the tracks, the 11:25 express is coming through!"*

THE PLAY:　*Swing forearms vertically to simulate pistons. Move toward your partner in a straight line while making loud, rhythmic steam emission noises. Blow whistle before moving off again.*

51

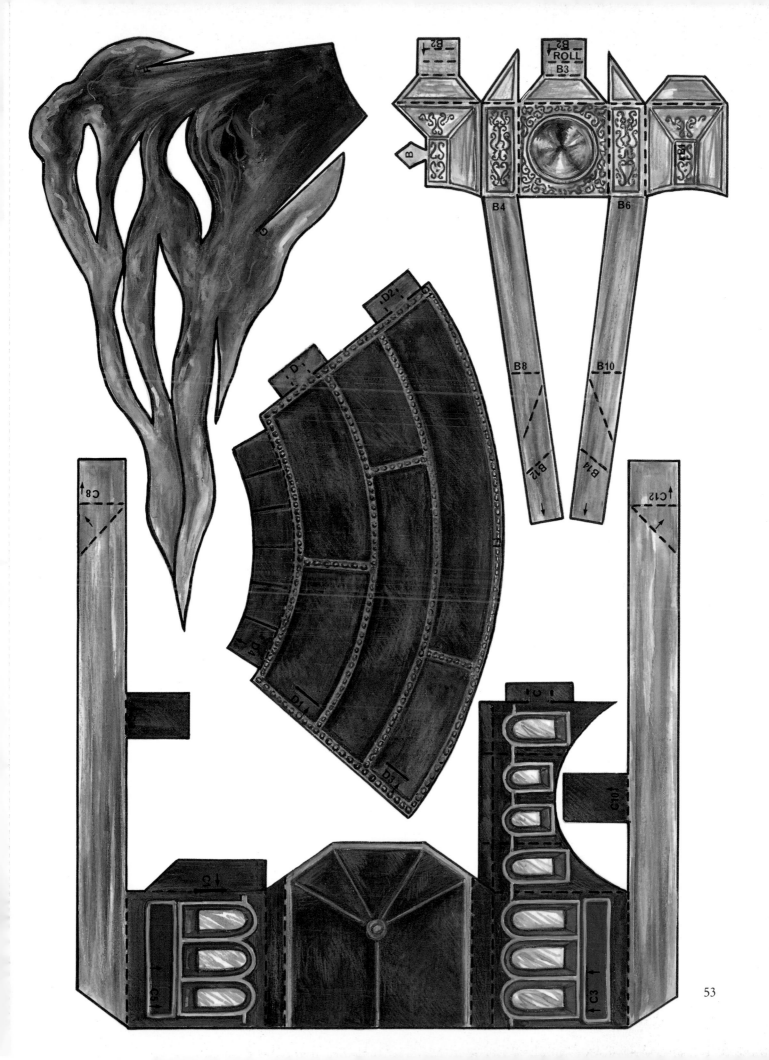

53

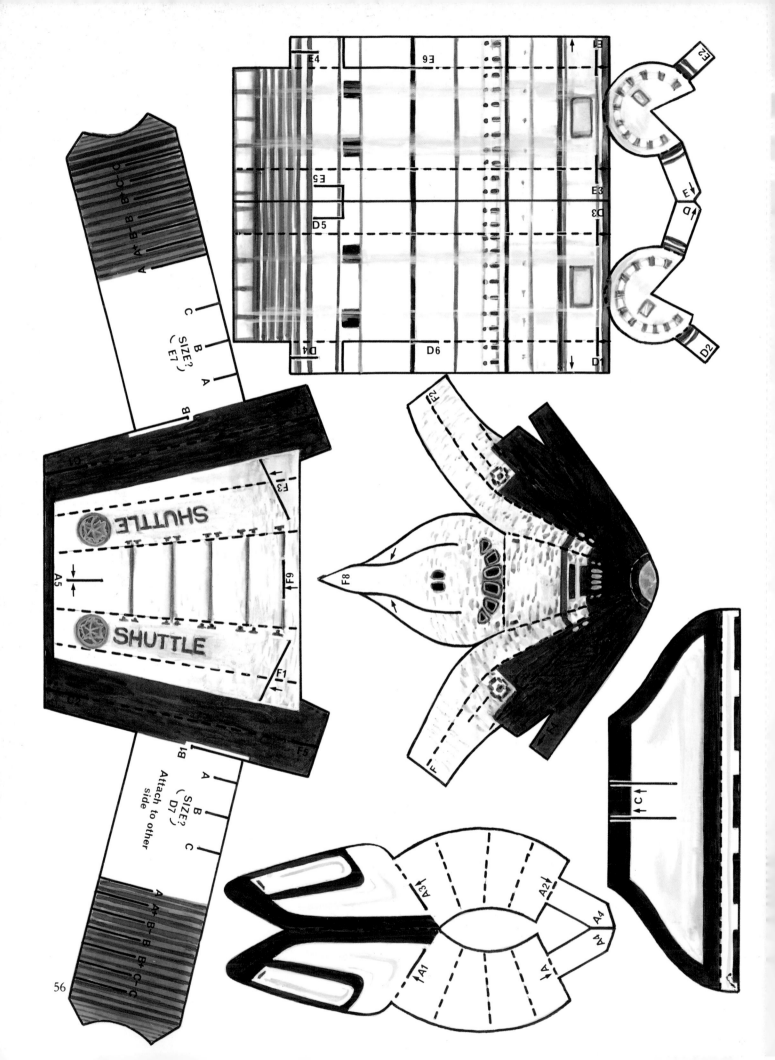

SHUTTLE

SHUTTLE

56

へ　ば
ざ　あ
あ　と
　　ん

紙茎

 SUPEHSU SHATORU : THE SPACE SHUTTLE

The Space Shuttle waits for the mighty rocket to carry it into the black silence of space. Rigid, swift, exploratory.

THE CALL: *"5...4...3...2...1...We have lift-off!"*

THE REPLY: *"This is Venus Base Station. Prepare for docking."*

THE PLAY: *Hold arms out from the body like delta wings, lean well forward and rush towards your partner making loud wooshing sounds. Later, swirl around silently as you go into orbit and prepare for re-entry.*

57

Shobosha

紙茎

へ ば あ
ざ あ
あ と
ば ん

SHOBOSHA : THE FIRE ENGINE

台詞

With lights flashing and siren wailing the Fire Engine speeds towards the big fire. Urgent, important, gushing.

THE CALL: *"Weeeeeooooo! Clear the way! Put up the ladder! Turn on the hose!"*

THE REPLY: *"Oh put me out! Put me out!"*

THE PLAY: *Hold one hand on top of the head and open and close it to simulate the flashing light. With the other hand pretend to hold the steering wheel and rush round your partner in ever decreasing circles. On reaching "the fire" put up the ladder.*

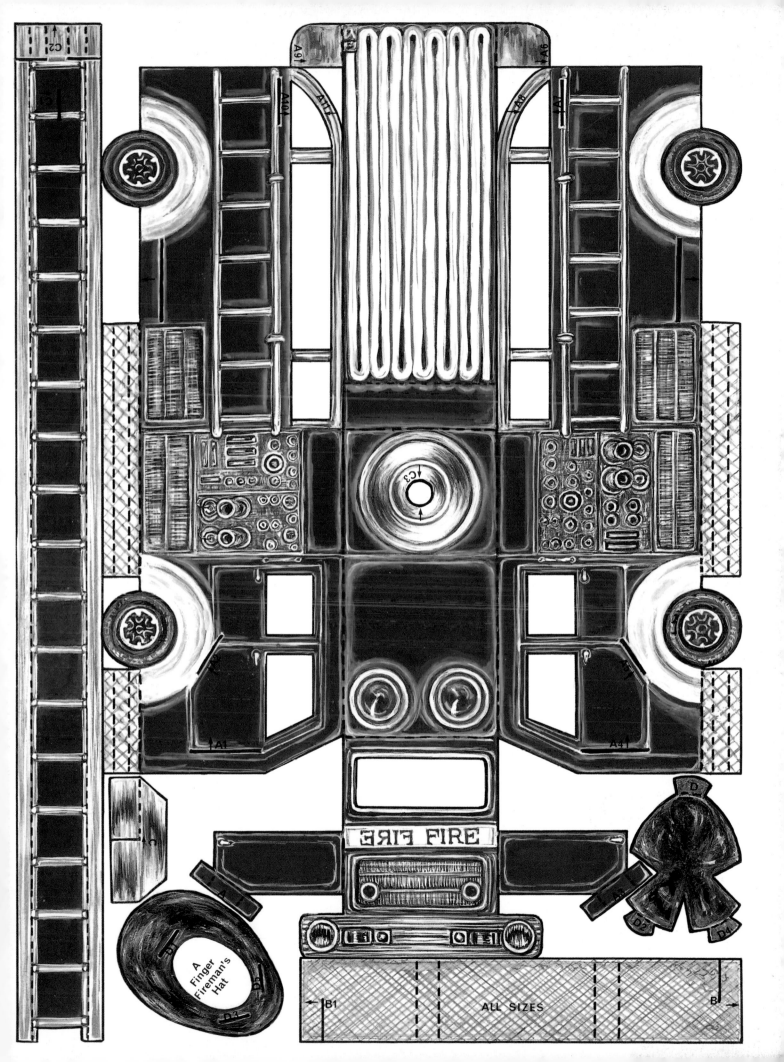

Shiritsu-Tantei

紙茎

へざあ ばあとん

SHIRITSU TANTEI : THE PRIVATE INVESTIGATOR

Ever watchful, the Private Dick lurks just out of sight, always ready for action. Cool, calm, tough.

THE CALL: *"If you want a quick solution we're going to have to move fast!"*

THE REPLY: *"That's fine by me. You got any clues?"*

THE PLAY: *With shoulders hunched and hands deep in pockets, saunter forward. If things get tricky shoot first and ask questions later.*

63

■ *Biographical Notes*

Heather Busch and Burton Silver are New Zealanders who share a unique vision engendered by that country's remote geographical location and its sensuous landscape. They arrived at their intense interest in Kokigami by very separate paths, one biological and the other spiritual, each representing the twin aspects of this special art.

Burton Silver is well known for his conservation work with hedgehogs and especially for the very successful "Hedgehog Corking Scheme." In order to prevent these creatures from drowning in private swimming pools, he developed a simple method of providing them with permanent floatation by sticking corks onto their prickles. Anyone who is involved with this painstaking task, as thousands are in New Zealand, will understand how it naturally led to a fascination with the sticking on of a variety of other things.

Heather Busch was drawn to an appreciation of the intimate art of the little paper costume by a more aesthetic route. While she is best known for her paintings of extremely old cats, it was an attempt to find new directions in stained glass sculpture that led to her study of the ancient Oriental art of Kokigami. A long time practitioner of body enhancement techniques, she was quick to realise that glass was an inappropriate medium and soon became expert in the design and decoration of lighter and safer paper sculptures. Her work, always tender and radiant with a definite frontal rigidity, now ranks alongside that of Yukiyujo in Japan and Carotte in France.